THE ROMAN BOOK
OF GARDENING

The Roman Book of Gardening brings together an extraordinarily vivid selection of texts on Roman horticulture, celebrating herb and vegetable gardening in verse and prose spanning five centuries. In an anthology of vivid new translations by John Henderson, Virgil's *Georgics* stand alongside neglected works by Columella, Pliny, and Palladius, bringing to life the techniques and obstacles, delights and exasperations of the Roman gardener. For all the cultural differences, modern gardening enthusiasts will recognize much of the familiar heaving and chopping that the writers describe but may be surprised at other aspects of horticulture that have changed significantly over the centuries.

This is a timely and valuable contribution to our understanding of gardening history, Roman culture and Latin literature. *The Roman Book of Gardening* is the first book on the practice of Roman gardening and includes a full Index of plants, listing names in both English and Latin, the language of botany.

John Henderson is Reader in Latin Literature, University of Cambridge, and Fellow of King's College, Cambridge. Among his books on Classics are *Classics: A Very Short Introduction* (1995 with Mary Beard), *Fighting for Rome: Poets and Caesars, History and Civil War* (1998) and *Writing Down Rome: Comedy, Satire and Other Offences* (1999).

Plate 1 Parham Park, West Sussex: End of day, potting shed corridor.

THE ROMAN BOOK
OF GARDENING

John Henderson

Routledge
Taylor & Francis Group

LONDON AND NEW YORK

First published 2004
by Routledge
11 New Fetter Lane, London EC4P 4EE

Simultaneously published in the USA and Canada
by Routledge
29 West 35th Street, New York, NY 10001

Routledge is an imprint of the Taylor & Francis Group

© 2004 John Henderson

Typeset in Garamond by
Florence Production Ltd, Stoodleigh, Devon
Printed and bound in Great Britain by
TJ International Ltd, Padstow, Cornwall

British Library Cataloguing in Publication Data
A catalogue record for this book is available from the
British Library

Library of Congress Cataloging in Publication Data
A catalog record for this book has been requested

ISBN 0–415–32449–1 (hbk)
ISBN 0–415–32450–5 (pbk)

CONTENTS

Everything in the garden

ILLUSTRATIONS

NOTE ON THE TEXT

In the **translations**, I have inset, at times interposing 'NB', material which in my view reads best as 'aside', 'footnote', or some other variety of para-textual item.

Dates in this book are all CE – unless marked BCE.

Measurements are given modern equivalents in English in the *Index: General Topics* – in the entry for 'measurements'.

For us, thanks largely to Linnaeus' classification system, **Latin** is for ever the official language of **botany**, so a full Index of plants, is provided, by Latin and English names. Naturally, linguistic translation never can neatly dovetail with cultural translatability, however much modern scientists may wish otherwise: to follow this up, see *Further Reading: General* – the entries for Stearn and Waquet.

In the notes, I have abbreviated our selection of authors as follows:

C.   =   Columella;
P.   =   Pliny;
Pall. =   Palladius;
V.*G*. =   Virgil, *Georgics*.

Plate 2 Relief panel from a funerary pillar. Musée Luxembourgeois, Arlon. Second sectury CE. On the left, breaking ground with a hoe, to the right, trenching with a long-handled, gripless spade.

PREFACE
Preparing the ground

The Roman Book of Gardening brings together the Latin texts which teach and celebrate herb and vegetable gardening in verse and prose. There are plenty of fascinating studies of Roman gardens, but this is the only book of Roman garden*ing*. The selections differ widely and wildly from one another, but in each of them the voice of the gardener, the gardener who means it, keeps ringing through. You can't miss it, outlook and attitude both add up – they are what make gardeners worth their salt. The first and last lesson will be that Roman gardening did not bother putting on airs. Our texts are in fact all sub-divisions within supposedly much grander projects.

I

The first part of wisdom is to *evaluate the actual person you mean to instruct*. The farmer designer must *not* compete with the rhetoric teacher's eloquence techniques, as has been done by most people – despite the fact they are speaking eloquently to country folk, they have managed to make their teaching unintelligible even to the most eloquent.

> – But let me *cut back* the delay that a *preface* is, and *not* imitate the ones I'm ticking off.

I must, if heaven favours, discuss all agriculture, pasturage, country buildings (in accordance with professors of architecture), water supply – every category of operation where a farmer must create or nurture, with a view to pleasure and profit. But with all things at their own season, marked out separately through the whole calendar. For sure, I have decided to keep to the format of going through *all* the instruction on each species *under the month for its planting*.

Palladius, *World of the Countryside* (1.1)

Palladius' gutsy approach to farming surges through this no-nonsense declaration of intent. He was right to be proud of producing the first 'month-by-month' calendar of tasks on the farm.

Living through the fifth century's precarious wind-down of the global supremacy of the Roman Empire, Palladius concentrates on the matter in hand, giving us no fix at all on the author but instead focusing all the attention on his plain man's work-chart. After an initial programme of general orders, he devotes a brisk and clearcut book to each month, working systematically through the list of sub-departments on the farm. Thus garden instructions come roughly half-way through (at section 14 of 23) *January*, and so it goes, through the year, to Book 13 and December.

Each batch of timely work on the garden tells us to *use* this text. Of course we must *read* it if we are to use it, but this is a 'manual', and wants green and grubby fingers to begrime its pages. On strides Palladius, tugging readers through the yearly cycle of gardening, with the minimum of fancy footwork and fussy writing. Yet his *Preface*'s scorn for mystifying rhetoric also has its pull on us: he is surely inviting us to warm to his own writing as we go, reading and weeding through the year. The *World of the Countryside* will indeed come across as a feat of efficient compactness, masterful economy, muscular *Latin*, for all the bizarre counsels of despair and unreason that his collection of wacky remedies and primitivesque rituals piles on the lucked-out gardener. The lore and the know-how rest on a half-dozen centuries of Roman experience – we can be sure he has read all the texts collected in this book, and many more besides. If you read through the chapters in order, you will recognize plenty of stuff from Columella and Pliny when you arrive at Palladius' synthesis in the final chapter.

The rest of *my* preface goes back to the beginning, to introduce the texts in chronological sequence. In the finale, Palladius' standing orders on each month's horticulture are brought together from their original locations, where they are filed in the middle of the procession of urgent appointments all over the farm. Our first text, which will serve as *Introduction*, also subordinates the garden as, apparently, a 'minor' activity among the many calls on the farmer's time. But this time, we are dealing with a very different writer. This time it is Rome's greatest poet who puts gardening in its place.

II

Virgil's classic *Georgics* marked the critical moment of permanent transformation for Roman politics. It was penned within a supportive circle around Maecenas, the closest adviser of Octavian Caesar, in the late 30s BCE, when the superpower Rome had staggered towards a full-scale showdown between Julius Caesar's son and heir, and his best general and lieutenant, Mark Antony. As Antony and Cleopatra killed themselves in defeat and despair in Egypt after the decisive battle of Actium in Greece (31 BCE), so Virgil intimates at the end of his poem, the poet was busy at work, 'flowering', as he puns, in the congenial surroundings of calm Naples, disengaged from the world state's affairs, detached from fame and glory. All the same, his work was finished in time to meet the deadline of Octavian's triumph in 29 BCE, and played its part in formulating, urging, and eternalizing, the message that this historic moment was to draw a line under civil strife, and usher in a permanent peace, under the aegis of a divinely blessed 'first citizen'. Swords into ploughshares. Army camps full of hardened veterans into pensioned-out parcels of farmland . . .

For good. As Octavian and his ministers settled to devising a system for this new world 'after politics', marked by his own rebranding as the emperor 'Augustus' (meaning 'the spirit of blessed increase'), the Mediterranean did indeed see redundant ex-soldiers by the thousand shipped out to vast new state-sponsored colonies in Spain, Africa, France, Greece, and way out east into the upland interior of Turkey. The poem seizes on its occasion.

In four power-packed books, Virgil explores the facets of humanity that are brought out by the work of farming: the primal struggle of the ploughman with the soil; and all the tribulations that keep the final harvesting of grain crops in the balance, no matter how careful and prudent the farming, until all is safely gathered in. Then the fiendish complications and subtleties of the cultivation of trees – vine, olive, orchard fruits, and the rest of the shrubs and bushes we commandeer and exploit. How many tiny yet impactful adjustments to the rich plantlife brought together from all across the known world had been made by the intuition, experimental flair, and dogged persistence, of growers down the years. Tending and intervention, breeding and grafting – so many activities that catch the collective project of civilization realized as productivity. Next there is livestock: in the relations between man and domesticated, farmyard, animals – horse, cow, sheep, dog – the farmer acts out the full range of roles, from playing god to suffering comrade, as these creatures move in and out of focus as vital produce on legs/as our partners in life – sharing our space, with many drives and instincts in common, and the same risks that afflict us, from birth to plague. Virgil's fourth and last book turns to beekeeping, source of sweetness in the classical diet, and irresistibly evocative site for the imaging of human culture. Honey-bees are by way of playing 'farmers' themselves, as they crop nectar from the flowers and process it in their 'natural' factory. In farming their hives, human beings superintend a 'farm' that is already a working society, incorporating within one organic space the microscopic equivalent of the human city with its hinterland of working farms such as supplied every 'Rome'. Seen up close through the eye of the keeper, the miracle of honey dramatizes a 'working model' of a world supremely geared to work. We direct, not just inspect, this, and know it to be less, and more, than ours is, or can be. Most particularly, Virgil's poetry catches and transmits the intricate, delicate minutiae of the bee's world of bright colour and swooning scent. His own productivity is enacted through the transformative work of his writing, the delicious distillation of ideas, feelings, and language.

It is in this context that the master poet of Rome writes us his vision of gardening. Virgil will go on to secure for himself, for all time, the status of centrepoint and paragon of Latin culture, by writing the vast poem of Roman destiny, the *Aeneid*, where the city of Rome takes centre-stage – its myth, legend, history, politics, ideology, self-image. At that point, the *Georgics* itself was subsumed within the works of Virgil, for his posthumous epic exploring the epoch-making triumph of Caesar Augustus' re-foundation of Rome – *imperial* Rome, *cosmopolis* – has been preserved ever since as *the* sacred text of Roman civilization. The *Georgics* even owe their preservation to the epic's incomparable prestige.

But where, then, is Virgil's gardening? A truly unforgettable glimpse is all he allows himself. And us. As the *Fourth Georgic* whirls him onwards, the poet takes pains to mark out the garden as a lamentable, regretted, *gap* in his poem on farming. He proffers gardening to us as a topic clamouring for posterity to prioritize. Make good the void left to glare from Virgil's farm. It is perfectly true that the ancient commentary on Virgil tells us that a certain Quintus Gargilius Martialis (a lost third-century writer) turned out to be the one destined to step into this breach. And (as we shall see) Columella *would* be devastated, after all his hard work – all that *gardening* – in trumpeting so loud that *his* garden would be following Virgil's instructions. But there is no call to regret what might have been. Rather, it will leap from the page (I guarantee) that there is *plenty* of gardening for us to read in the *Georgics*. Virgil's *idea* of a 'gap' is the point. He is telling us to think where the garden *belongs* on the farm.

His own strategy is to put horticulture in a corner. A *special* corner. To one side, a protected patch where the flowers can feed the bees. Where ancient culture found sweetness, concentrated. Here the poet's honeyed words *sample* gardening for us all. His bid to memorialize, in a flash, the classical tradition of the garden of poetry takes the form of a startling cameo. He prepares the way by thrusting at us the topic of 'rosebeds at Paestum', where blooms come twice in the year. An icon of paradise that surely pictures the redoubled fertility of Virgil's combination of text and topic – we glimpse the book *and* the gardening. The momentary scene he goes on to feature will talk up, in haunting Graeco-Roman mythic terms, a sideline spot at mild, temperate Tarentum, in the corner of southern Italy.

Here Greek culture had once clashed, but long since blended, with Rome. Virgil's Latin landscape evokes the long tradition of Greek poetry, animated as a wizened Old Gardener devotedly tending his beloved plants. All the cultural work embodied in the *Georgics*, on paper and in heads, is evoked by this magical parable – checking out the values and scale of agrobusiness against the caring intimacy of gardening. It takes no time at all – explicit sermonizing would undo the point – and, besides, herbs, veg., flowers, and a bit of fruit are all a poem needs to grow. Light as you please, Virgil's story tells how his gardener gave him eyes to see, and he challenges us to follow his lead.

III

Columella, most industrious and tenacious of writers, came from Spain to farm and write near Rome, at work on his *Country Life* perhaps from the 40s to the early 60s. (At no point do the tragicomic reigns of Claudius and Nero intrude on the scene.) He has more to say on gardening than the rest of classical antiquity put together – literally more, in quantity, but also and more to the point, *more to the point*. His *poem* on the garden in 436 hexameters bursts into the monumental prose manual as its Book 10. It is regularly read as a free-standing composition, and grabs what little attention Columella's gardening has commanded. But we shall take first the dry-eyed prose presentation in **Columella Eleven**, which runs down a fully detailed programme of instruction for you to give your farm manager. (He already knows it all from experience, but you can keep up the pretences and tell him by the book.) The vegetables and herbs which starred in the poem just before recur, but the professional style and professorial persona of Books 1 to 9 are back in charge again. Why the switch? So that we can first connect with the world of canny, applied know-how of garden-lovers everywhere. After that, by all means, the poem can cut loose with its release of whooping enthusiasm and emotional highs and lows through every turn of the garden. (You wait.)

Gardening begins with the garden, and the garden begins (Virgil made us see it this way) with its framing enclosure. Gardeners must 'keep out people and animals'. Hence the low-cost and indestructible 'living hedge' of thorn. Once that is settled, we can get on with choice of site: beside the farmhouse; soil quality: rich; and water supply – a stream abutting, or else a well. Negatively: no garden must lie below a threshing-floor. Now we have our garden space, preparations for sowing can begin: watering as, when, and where need be, digging over, muckspreading, and 'once for all, at every moment in time, plan to get rid of weeds'. These are essential preliminaries to spring and to autumn sowing alike. Some species sow at both seasons, others only in the autumn. More precisely, the gardener needs to run down, month by month, which species sow best when, from January to August (for all that only parsley/celery is on between the end of April and the tail end of August).

But gardening – gardening always breaks down operations to *specifics*. Horticulture means getting to grips with individual plant care. They are all different, they have their own ways. Garlic, cabbage, lettuce, leeks/chives, asparagus, cucumber/gourd, onion, navew/turnip/radish . . . – these are the complicated, tricky, ambitious, cussed ones. Dotted in among them are the short and sweet propositions, requiring their own customized entries: artichoke, mustard, coriander, rocket, basil, all-heal, celery/parsley, parsnip/carrot, rampion, elecampane, alexanders, mint, rue, thyme and savory, pepperwort, beet, chervil and orach, poppy, dill, caper.

'At this point end the instructions which are in Columella's opinion needed on Garden Care.' And at this point, too, he gives us to understand, end the instructions which are in Columella's opinion needed on the whole *World of the Countryside*. For Book 11 ends with what must come across as the firmest conclusion to a text that you could wish for, announcing 'an appendix containing the *Topics of All Columella's Books*. As and when the need arises, finding what to look for in each book, and how to deal with each problem, will easily be possible.'

A full list of 'Contents' duly runs down books 1–11. But then comes a jolt. An extra 'Contents' heads yet one more book – *Twelve*. On the one hand, it all adds up to an *extremely* coherent overall reference system. One which makes Columella, and he would preen if he knew it, the most consultable classical text to have come down to us. On the other, just where Columella puts his gardens in his *World of Country Life* defines his take on gardening. It says how he means horticulture to gear in with the larger enterprise, to make up an effective programme of teaching. So let's see.

Gardening is so special in Columella it grabs a whole, unique, book of deviation from the manual's prose. And it is special, too, because it gets a *second* outing, in prose, as the final section of Book 11. Yet the index passes up on gardening, and on gardening alone, for both the poetry book, *Ten*, and also for our gardening section in *Eleven*, with its plant-by-plant course of focused entries. Each species got its moment of full attention there, then on to the next – the next write-up. So why wasn't the gardening worth proper accessing?

We must go back over the sequence. The last words of *Nine* came as a mighty shock:

> But now that discussion of the farmhouse animals and their feeding has reached completion, the remaining section of *Countryside Matters* (below), namely: *Horticulture*, Silvinus, shall next, as both you and our friend Gallio co-plotted, be processed into **Columella in Verse**. ||

As we shall see, the prose preface to *Ten* at once confirmed, and explained, this bombshell: the manual was substantially complete *according to the traditional definition* of the task; but the garden had become a 'modern' pre-occupation, and demands/deserves proper handling. If a job is worth doing, it's worth doing properly.

Eleven, titled 'The Farm Manager', is a further jolt: Book 10 ended with no sign of anything more to come. But the new preface puts us straight: Columella was already down to do gardening in prose, for a certain 'Claudius, an imperial priest', when the whole work's overall addressee Silvinus burst on the scene along with a new figure, Gallio, to outbid him. *Eleven* will now supplement both the earlier discussion of the Manager in Book 1 and the Garden of Poetry in *Ten* – 'so long as Silvinus agrees' with the idea. This manoeuvring tells us that this is a special patch; but the presence of Silvinus reassures us that it belongs to the overall project. These gardens may have been pushed to the back of the queue; yet they may be the stars of the entire show.

Columella's job description for the Manager moves from the general run of duties on to a steadily more insistent focus on the paramount importance of their correct *timing*. Time of year, time of day, workdays and festivals, constant . . . vigilant . . . diligence must radiate from him through all the staff, and counter those eternal enemies, 'ignorance and negligence'. 'As in the rest of life', but 'especially in farming', these foes do more harm than knowledge does good. 'Who could doubt how time's runaway train cannot be caught?'. The ancient bard Hesiod was so right in telling us 'He who hesitates is lost'. No wonder countryfolk mutter 'Don't hesitate to sow', for if you don't get jobs done on the day for them – 'on *their* day' – then 'Not the dozen daylight hours of one day but a whole year is dead'. If one job is done 'late', then the whole cycle will be 'late', and this 'cheats the hopes of a whole year'. . . . I think we get the point.

This barrage of hectoring voices ushers in a monthly rota for the Manager's duties. He must know the stars and sky, but farming is applied science, not slide-rule mechanics – using nous, forethought, and multi-vectored reckoning to adapt general truths to particular prevailing conditions. Maybe this will be the year when spring came early – there's to be no waiting till the stars come right. The precise almanac that follows, running from 13 January right round the calendar to 12 January, insists from the outset that farming can start before spring *if the timing is right*.

On the way, the gardener's year is held over for separate treatment: as we have seen, it is organized as a full account of gardening from first principles, from the 'living hedge' onward. True, once the imaginary plot is sorted, the first section groups tasks in preparation for the sowing season – of early spring. Columella gets us into weeding, muckspreading, second digging five days before sowing time, and orders beds 'divided up' around mid January, to kick in with precise instructions for sowing. With the complication that gardens sow in autumn as well as spring, he does give a monthly run-down, in less than 150 words, for those sowing times between January and August; but this is still preliminary to the main action – the full treatment required by each plant species in its own right.

So *Eleven* takes the garden out of Columella's diary of farm management, but still tackles it as a pressing challenge to formulate a working annual *timetable*. It works with the presumption that the knowledge that has been applied to the farm still applies behind that hedge; but it insists that the focus of attention must change inside the enclosure. This gardening is a matter of man-, as well as plant-, management.

Twelve will rub this in. Titled 'Farm Manageress', to make a pair – an asymmetrical pair, but still a pair – with the 'Manager' of *Eleven*. He must keep an eye on Her, since She is His 'helper' in and about the farm-house, but the overall responsibility is His. Yet this *is* Her special sphere of supervision. Her domain. The staff bring closure to the entire manual, and everything now steadily (and literally) homes in on the farmhouse 'larder'. Manageress moves steadily through the farm and garden calendar, the work determined by the time of year when produce became available for reception at the farmhouse. She does not need to look out for the vagaries and uncertainties of stars and weather, for she must take on, and take in, what she is given, and deal with it.

Her first job is just the same as the farmer's and the gardener's: 'preparation' – getting the place and the utensils 'ready for preserves'. We get her recipes for vinegar and for hard brine, the two main preservative media. This readies her for the spring equinox, when 'herbs need gathering and storing' – all the pickling she can squeeze from the garden: 'sprouts, cabbage, caper, parsley/celery stalks, rue, alexanders bloom and stalk, same for fennel and wild carrot/parsnip, white bryony flower, asparagus, butcher's broom, white vine, houseleek, pennyroyal, cat mint, charlock, samphire . . .'. 'All these are preserved by the same preservative'. Spring gives way to summer between lettuce and onions. Fruit now demands timely provision of the sweet preservative, honey. Cheese takes us to August's apples and figs, for drying and storing, before we run into vintage and the end of summer, with a tailpiece on raisins. The 'processing' of autumn produce 'swells the demands on her'. There are the pomegranates to see to. Fruit and the awkward herb elecampane take her up to winter and oliveage. With the new year, our housekeeper is busy making more oil, salting the pork, pickling navew and turnip whether from farm or garden, and in January to February, finally pulling the rest of the garden herbs – mustard, alexanders, and rampion – and activating Columella's recipes for salads (savory, mint, rue, coriander, parsley, chives or onion, lettuce, colewort, thyme, cat mint, pennyroyal . . . with nuts, or cheese . . .). To help deal with all the *World of the Countryside*, a final digestive or two (white pepper, parsley seed, silphium, cheese; or lovage, raisins, dried mint, pepper . . .).

The message becomes more and more pronounced. Manageress is here to 'receive, take in, store/preserve, keep safe, make long lasting, stop the rot', *all* the produce from *all* the departments of the farming operation. Pickling, seasoning, fermenting, potting, sealing – her kitchen and its larder spell *closure* for Columella's diligent storehouse of memory. She is like the 'gleucine oil' which she gets on with towards the end, when it was *reserved* for this part of the book, though it does not belong to this part of the year, so as not to interrupt the wine-making. She, too, was herself '(p)reserved' for this final moment, all her own. That living hedge behind us, hers is the last *enclosure* – the cupboard door Columella shuts on *his* well-stocked archive.

Now we can see what Columella's three 'late arrivals' have in common: the dynamics of the multi-culture which is characteristic of the herb and vegetable plot. His earlier books could cover vast tracts of land with furrow and corn, vine and olive, horse and cow, sheep and goat . . . and even bees and game could be dealt with 'in the round', one item, species, or variety at a time. But running the garden combines that attuned sensitivity required of the gardener who means to tend the various plants successfully, with the organized efficiency of 'his better half's' kitchen and outhouse skills. The endlessly varied and individualized blends of pickling agent, flavouring, ingredients, container, and store. In both cases, the specifics of each plant's expected and actual life-cycles, vulnerabilities, resiliences, preferences, tolerances, and so on, create complex challenges. There are so many bioclocks to synchronize. There are no heroics, just timetabling and technique. Just jam.

So it is that the work of gardening takes its place out back of Columella's farm, a vital part of it actually done *indoors*. Horticulture is agriculture and arboriculture writ small – but it is a concentrated replica of the whole; an intense, intensive, fraction. *Eleven* celebrates the passionate cult of timing, and the profusion of growing methods, as dictated by these so many different subjects. What verse will bring the garden of *Ten* is intensified, graphic, 'flowery' *writing*. The stunning poetry that describes the work and skill of the gardener goes hand in glove with the heartfelt work of the gardener, which in turn pushes the reader to get into the poet's flamboyant work, and join in.

IV

Columella's prose version of Roman gardening, and its rivals, are trained on utility, mastering the environment, trading technical mastery between their own performance and the skills they describe – between verbiage and herbage. The flowery burst of hothouse enthusiasm in **Columella Ten** will instead jazz up the veg. and herb patch – into a cosmic 'rite of spring', where Mother Earth has hair-raising sexual relations with seed and plant, and the pursuit of paradise takes an orgiastic turn.

We *were* prepared for Columella's surprise leap onto the high-flying trapeze of poetic acrobatics. In the time-honoured pattern, ploughland had led on to arboriculture, then a stupendously lavish vineyard, olives, fruit-trees, and shrubs, in three packed tomes. Two books on stock, with appropriate veterinary medicine, tackled first cattle, horse, and mule, then 'minor', smaller, animals – sheep, goats, pigs, farm dogs. And Books 8 and 9 reviewed livestock at the farmhouse – aviary and fishpond; game-run and apiary. The book of bees ends (we saw) with the surprise promise of flowers – in verse. The logic is inescapable: arable crops were primal, with those titanic struggles to break and work the earth, the heave of heavyweight oxen, the grand scale of furrowed fields stamping the land with human willpower and expertise. Vineyard, olive grove, fruit-orchard are extensive, too, spectacular alteration of the face of the earth. They involve collective ingenuity, infinitely scrutinized finesse, and miracles of intervention on natural resources; but no one could argue that they could come *before* grain. Fruit is, for ever, afters – a riot of culture. Columella, he says, can graft *anything on anything*. Roman animals sort themselves into descending sizes. Mammals first, then down the scale to fish and fowl. The question for the agro-text had always been: how far to push – what prize coverage, let alone *completeness*? Game reserve? Hives? Garden?

11

At the garden gate of *Ten's* preface, Columella waves at us that he follows Virgil's hives with the flowers marked out in *Georgic* 4 as extruded from his Farm. He had begun to train for his maiden flight when he first turned to bees, in *Nine*. He revved up the writing, with a grand run of 'authorities' featuring the busy bee scholar Hyginus, but starring Virgil's 'flowery poetic'. For, he pirouetted, bees attract all the sweet nonsense of mythology, Greek-style. True, bees live in a walled enclosure, in a flower garden of their own, with running water, at a nice spot: bees, in short, are more farming. But that's not all. Bees are also 'gardeners' in *their* garden, and they make/let Columella write *differently*. Behind that hedge, he gets ready to *fly*.

So it is that the indefatigable applied agriculturalist pupates into an enthused poet-priest of cosmic ecstasy. Columella *Ten* singles gardening out as the hotbed of existence. Enter the gate, and find paradise: leave again, and re-enter reality. The rest of the *World of the Countryside* encrypted, and will seal up again, the lyrical fantasia that bursts onto the page in its garden – but the hard work that lies behind every blossom is honoured, too, in every forcing line of luscious audacity. Gardeners are not in the habit of showing it, but emotional over-investment in our plant successes and failures does earn every whoop and groan Columella's histrionics can come up with. Just this once, mind.

For sure, the poem is structured as a year-round sequence, starting in autumn just after the vintage when a farmer can find a spot of time for his garden; starting in autumn so the poem can climax in rampant Bacchic revel, a festal text triumphant. The calendar will mix and maul stars, weather, festivals, months, gods, myths, rustic formulae, quotation, and allusion to classic verse. Pumping the tone, overloading the atmospherics. Pressing for response more than pacing and pegging out the round of duties. If you please, souping up the myth proves gardening always was as grand a theme as any epic thundering.

The pyrotechnics are dazzling. They shoot off, rapid-fire. So **Columella Ten** will grow plenty of explanatory notes. It will be a good idea for me to give an 'advance' on the translation in store. The tonal run of the poem needs to be grasped, and I think it best if I let you see how compulsive it can get right away. There is no chance of spoiling the effect. Frankly, I don't think you will believe that Columella said any such thing, until you read it for yourself. But I should wind you up ready, anyhow.

The teeming space for what Columella calls his 'garden symphony' is first envisaged, enclosed, and established, like the garden in *Eleven*, and like the farm and its sub-divisions from Book 1 on. Where the other allotment used Virgil's 'feast that cost nowt' for its opening tag (11.3.1 ~ *Georgic* 4.133), *Ten* splashes affiliation to Virgil all over its entrée. This will be a *Fifth Georgic* from start to finish. Columella will season his *Georgics* produce, as Virgil had before him, with a sprinkling of sensual bounty from Virgil's first gems, the exquisite pastoral *Eclogues*. He will fool with Virgil's national epic, too, as Virgil could not, and have gardening take on empire-building, and walk off with the prize . . . fruit and veg. The power of herb, the glory of spray.

A poem needs a god to watch over it: crude but seminal Priapus stands proud at the centre of Columella's garden:

> Phallic fright. Eternal presence. A garden's focal point.
> Groin to menace the boy, the burglar shooed by his sickle.

But make no mistake, this is poetry, so Muses must be invoked, too, the fuss of poetic finesse advertised as the point of our exercise:

> Pierian sisters, channel the song fine. Columella's Muses.

'Winter preparations' tap into awful reserves of energy, plenty of voltage to launch the bard. The gardener's sky is full of dangerous astral vermin, strange monsters come to the rescue, and we are heading for the first salvo from the poet's arsenal of almighty shocks in making gardening weird, wonderful, and – primeval. Here in dead of winter, picture the poet-gardener's first tangle with work as a horrible mutilation of our Hesiodic mother, Earth. *Dig her.* Right inside. Two feet down. Columella raises the spectre so as to banish its nightmare. Greek Myth says Prometheus first fashioned earthenware humans, from clay plus water; but then Myth wiped us out in the Flood, so our lot only start with Deucalion and Pyrrha casting stones that came alive and restocked the planet. Columella takes off, and outbids, the violent heaves and switches of mythographic poetry, as he gets ready to push and squeeze the conceptual outcome of using personificatory imagery for working the soil. This first blitz hits us before we can take cover – but he means to take the themes of gardening as matrix of love-and-hate to unthinkable extremes. Bash her in, tear her out, turn her over. You know what spadework on a wintry day can be like. Bloody (but) exhilarating.

Rude awakenings are a perennial tactic of didactic poetry. Come February, and the Lyre constellation sets, and our bard is set to lower the tone: what, on earth, is about to . . . hit the fan? 'Don't be ashamed of rich dung and foul ash', as farmer Virgil had soon told *his* ploughboys:

> Then a fattening cake is the thing: ass dung, say, in lumps,
> or cowpat. Feed the ravenous earth till it wants no more.
> The gardener *does it himself*. Basket straps snap with the load.
> Get your fresh-ploughed fallow fed. There is no call for shame.
> All the sewage toilets spew out, from the pipelines of filth.

Soon enough, the gardener's digging and hoeing will break down his violent midwinter erotics into a hypertrophic, hyper-tropical, hothouse of voluptuous poetics. This gardening is, for once out loud, going to be an emotionally draining, and all-engrossing, love affair. First we move from soiled latrine to the sheen of spring. In a bright catalogue of floral tribute:

> Now. In all hues, paint the flowers – they are earth's own stars:
> Snowdrops in shimmering white. Burnished marigold-en eyes,
> etc.,
> etc.

A score of vegetables march past at the double, in a full scatter of broadcast seed, before Columella's New World symphonic poem, his Ode to Joy, stops the show:

> Share the moment, heavy sow the most prevalent of plants –

'Sing Cabbage'. The array of fifteen varieties takes our garden tour around central and southern Italy and back again, circling around Virgil's writing-den for the *Georgics*, at Naples, city of culture. And grand(iose) Virgil is misquoted and mock-quoted, for his *epic* catalogue of cabbages and kings, the fine crop of more or less native heroes with which Italy once 'flowered', when Trojan Aeneas came to chop them back.

But every spring's shower of Roman seed – of *semen* – makes Earth All Mother, all over again:

Just look! Mother so mild is out protesting for her brood,
she both wants the babies she bore, and she wants them right now,
and she asks for her step-children, too.

That is: sowing seed now goes ahead alongside shifting seedlings. Cue
for another coruscation:

All the myriad hues that ritzy Nature delivers,
a mosaic in plants, by the gardener who sowed them as seeds.

Exploding, this time, to fill the page with lush lettuces. By the lorry-
load: types from all over the Roman world, and the Roman archive: two
sorts named for a great Republican general; one from out east in Anatolia,
at one end of the earth, one from Columella's home town, Cadiz, at the
other. Sowing time for sexy-sounding Cypriot Paphian takes us out, and
into Venus' vernal month of April.

Venus' lettuce now hits that release button, or squeezes the trigger,
and sex detonates through the universe. Ocean and Neptune impregnate
their wives, the sea teems with life. Jupiter rides again, playing the shower
of rain trick he once used on Danae in myth – but this time he comes
down, not on some locked-up daughter, but on . . . Mother Earth. Our
bard peaks in a swoon of wonder, as the explosion of parent–child sex
hits the globe with new life, growth, spring again:

While the thing wants, looks to mate with, the mother who wants it,
and while that mother, so soft, lies there beneath giving ground,
germinate in her. Now is the cosmic mating season.
Now love spurts for intercourse. Now the spirit of the world
goes pell mell, raving for sex. Whipped then by lashings of lust
it falls in love with its children, fills them with pregnancies.

The psychobabble rhetoric of 'plenitude' has its moment – as poetic
amplification rams home the purple passage of desire, as promised, to
the hilt. Does the earth move for you? *It should*. Violence soaks the
screen, marked, again, in the order of mimesis, by the poet's own
irruption –

But why have I . . .

– for Columella just jumped the garden wall. He lost it, in that undi-
dactic paroxysm – he sounded like some demented, common or garden,
Lucretius, whose Epicurean philosophy of eternal genesis-decomposition
opens with a cosmic Hymn to Venus-as-Nature in spring spate, before
settling to hard analytic work through the postulates and riders of atomic
physics. Lucretius' massive poem could explain later how his Mother Earth
signifies, in the real, Materialist Matter. But Columella must get straight
back to work – figured as pruning and gardening, as he reins in, and gets
on with the work of planting and growing.

Before he lands, the reverie soars ever more stratospherically from
Apollo's Delphi, where the god's possessed priestess prophesied to the
world. Off on a Dionysiac freak-out into the wild 'beyond' – past the
Mother Goddess Cybele's home in Anatolia, where her worshippers must
castrate themselves in frenzied devotion to her. Following Dionysus'
vertiginous route all the way from his birthplace in Nysa, way out east,
to triumph over the city of Thebes, beneath spooky Mt Cithaeron, and
assume his rightful place beside Apollo at Delphi. To have his half of the
'Pierian, Parnassian' action of the Muses. Infusing Dionysus builds the
voice of praise into a howl of delight, sub-linguistic cries for Apollo 'Paean
of Delos', and Dionysus 'Paean of [yelps of adoration]'. Upon which,
Columella duly collapses, from this vertiginous fit of sublimity. From all
this unleashed *poetry*.

Just one Muse will do us proud, for our short trip around the garden;
for a song to work to – up in the trees, or . . . to come down to earth
again . . . down in the furrows, one man and his veg.:

> So come, on with the next. With dwarf gaps between each furrow,
> see that seed is broadcast . . .

This trough gets another crowd of species planted in these humble rows
of verse, before spring returns – nothing to stop our year turning, and
turning its page – for a second gasping wave of high-octane thrill. You
see, the flowers are ready to pick. Just think:

> Oyez, oyez. Harvest looms upon perfumed flowers: now.
> The radiant spring: now. The year's kaleidoscopic offspring
> paint mother's brow, and the make-over gladdens her [he]art: now.

Eyes open, jaw drops, girls blush, perfume as good as the Queen of Sheba's . . .

Now, Muses are girls, whichever way you look at it. More than less. Thus they are sisters — sisters to all the long list of sisters that throng the erotic landscapes of classical poetry. Including the friends of Ceres' daughter Proserpine, out flower-picking in Sicily when the god of Hell surfaced from Ovid's great epic of myth (and sex), to pick him a bride. She was kidnapped, raped, wed, and enthroned. Her mother gets her back, then loses her, annually. And that *is* our year, our allotment of seasons. Columella tries it on his chosen nymphs, the soft sell all over again: 'Trust me, gentle maidens, you are safe with me' . . .

Up at dawn to pick the buds, the poet goes back to (reawaken) what may be Virgil's earliest poem, where goatherd Corydon despairs of beloved Alexis' scorn. Another wild nymph, their 'Naiad', can come and fetch more baskets of flowers, to help Virgil's poem win the day, repair the hole in his poetry, and . . . ultimately make an old peasant a very happy man, safe behind a Virgilian hedge:

> You, too, Naiad, stop 'Alexis scorning Corydon's wealth',
> 'lovely as Alex is, you are lovelier still'.

Bundles of cut blooms in baskets. What poetry is, and does best. Colour, redolence, blend, weave, cumulation, distension, hyperinflation, and burst. But as the herbs are culled, pulled, torn, cut, chopped, and lifted — the sky darkens. We must make haste.

For it is a systemic syndrome of didactic poetry to tip in a trice from ripe acme over into crowding threat, lowering poison, rotting decay. We shall not save the poem from itself as it plunges towards its own winter extinction. From here on, the year runs away with us, for growing has to keep in step with time, even when it runs out.

Sheets of rain. Caterpillars and bugs. Rust and blight. Remedies, a potpourri of mumbo-jumbo. Taking the biscuit, in this cupboard-full of 'Etruscan' wizardry:

> . . . in case no treatment can fend off the infestation,
> then Dardanian techniques must come in. A woman must plant
> her bared feet, as her time comes, when a good heifer like her
> must serve natural law, and blood flows to her shame, unclean —

17

but she must walk free, loose at the breast, loose hair for last rites –
as thrice she is led round the beds, and hedge, of the garden.
Her step beats the bounds in lustration. Stupendous to see!
Just as when a tree gets a good shake, and a cloud rains down
of shiny round apples, say, or acorn's protective case.
Down on the ground roll torn bodies. Convulsed caterpillar.
So hypnotic spells once drugged the dragon, till it dropped off.
Slid down from Phrixus' fleece, so all of Iolcos could see.

Sex, caterpillars, videotape: and . . . cut. It's a wrap, of defamiliarized didactic making one last desperate shift at powering the essay, now that the flowers run out, and rot. *Fleurs du mal*:

But, it's time, the season to chop those early 'first-cut' stalks,
and tear off the stems . . .

of all those plants we have already written into the ground. Time to cut away from the recent run of quaint potions, and the overdone sequence of elaborate similes, run to stalk and seed. Perfect emblem of the poetics of luxuriance, now – watch out for the double act of cucumber and gourd. Through the rank bush and bristle creep and crawl this pair of fat-bellies, everything from fatal to life-saving, as versatile as Columella's verse, as necessary as his expertise. Fair and foul.

The Dog Star now arrives, to presage the closing of the circle from the poem's opening. There is just space/time for one more fresh topic. Fruit comes pelting down and piling up to fill a page with juice and plenty, and . . . still turnip is still going into the ground in late August. Yes, the planet's harvest of figs lifts one last wave of ecstasy, as Columella's vintage is due, praise be to Dionysus:

– But Columella's grapes are now ripe. Fearful lobbying
by 'Hosanna' Bacchus. Who tells us, horticulture is done.
We close the garden gate. We countryfolk heed your command.
So exultant we do harvest your blessings, sweet Bacchus.
Among rutting Satyrs. Among Pans half-human, half-goat.
Our arms wave now. They droop when the wine gets stale, and goes off.
'You, the Maenalian! You, Bacchus! You, the Lyaean! And you,
father, the Lenaean!' we hymn. Invite him into our home.

So the wine-tank ferments, filled with lakes of Falernian wine.
The vats will boil and bubble with rich new must. Overspill.

At this point, Woody, ends my lecture on horticulture . . .

taken from the 'ancient sources'. Hesiod through Virgil, through
Columella. The call has come, time we called Bacchus into our tanks,
vats, racks, cellar, stores.

What is a farm without fruit and veg.?
What are fruit and veg. without spice and herb?
What are herbs without honey, vinegar and brine, oil?
What is a garden without a gardening book?
What is gardening without Columella?
And what is *more* poetic than gardening?

V

Pliny's *Natural History* has a *Preface* plus thirty-seven volumes, the first
an index to the rest; it was completed in 77, two years before asthmatic
death by asphyxiation at the pyroclastic eruption of Vesuvius in 79 which
overwhelmed Pompeii and Herculaneum (Pliny the Younger, *Letters*
6.16). Pliny takes the universe to bits, or at least all the claims to knowledge of our world's properties and resources that he could glean from
whatever books he could lay hands on. **Book 19** showcases a detailed
analysis of the plants in the garden, for their physical properties as part
of the resources of the planet, interspersed with interesting details, and
. . . marvels. Pliny had read Columella, published some ten years earlier,
and has a very different take on the garden. (He cites him to *dis*agree:
17.51, 18.70, 303.) The garden is treated principally as a taxonomic set
of sets, and entrée to a wondrous 'pharmacy'. Precision wrestles with
gaffes, science with nonsense.

Pliny's own *Preface* calls itself 'Pliny on the pull', declaring the
mammoth compilation 'a job on the lighter side – no room for talent',
with 'barren ma(t)ter, Nature's procreation, Life', for story. He promises:

20,000 facts worth caring about – since, as Domitius Piso says,
store-houses a must, not books – from the reading of *c.* 2,000

volumes, and only pretty few of them touched by studious specialists because their contents are recondite, taken from a 100 author search, have been included in my 37 volumes, supplemented by a very large number of facts, either (a) unknown to predecessors, or (b) discovered later by Life.

His self-portrait of the artist as compulsive fact-collector comes next:

> We are human, and busy with duties, too, and care for this in 'set-aside' times, i.e. night-time, in case any of you thinks there's been easing down in those hours. We invest the days in all of you, we calculate health :: sleep, happy with just the one dividend, that, while we (as Varro puts it) 'hum-and-hah' over this stuff, we live extra hours. For a fact, life = being awake.

We don't believe a word of it when he tells the young prince and heir apparent Titus not to waste valuable time trying to read *Natural History*:

> Because for the public good I must go easy on the busy demands on you, the contents of individual books are subjoined to this letter from me, and with utmost care I have managed to eliminate your having them to read through. It will be you who by this device will empower others to avoid reading through, too, but as each one wants something, the question can be put, and it be known where to find it. This was done before me, in our literature, by Valerius Soranus, in the books entitled '*Mystery Priestesses*'.

But the best picture of this eccentric human volcano who wound up Grand Vizier of the Cosmos – Pliny at work – is given us by a *Letter* of his nephew, and adoptive son, 'Pliny the Younger', who takes eager readers on *A Library Tour Around My Uncle* (3.5):

Pliny to Friend Baebius Macer: Greetings

1   It is a great pleasure to me that you are reading away so earnestly at my uncle's books that you want to own them all and ask what they all are.

2   I shall play the role of catalogue, and, as well, I'll fill you in on the order they were written in. Yes, this is knowledge-acquisition that brings studious students no lack of delight.

3   'Mounting the Missile: On Equestrian Pride, 1 only.' Composed during tour as cavalry regimental officer.
= Talent + care combined 50/50.

'Biography of Pomponius Secundus, I + II.' Paid, so to speak, as service owed to memory of friend.
= Pliny uniquely loved by Pomponius.

4   'Wars in Germany, I–XX.' Compilation of all our wars *versus* Germans. Begun during tour in Germany. Inspiration < dream: in sleep, Drusus Nero likeness stood by (triumphant in Germany far and wide; *ob. ibid.*), entrusted + implored > rescue his memory from criminal oblivion.

5   'Studious Students, I–III (divided, on account of bulk, in *fasc.* I–VI).' Training manual for orators: starting from cradle > the full course > complete perfection.

'Dodgy Latin, I–VIII.' Written under Nero, his last years.
= Enslavement > every genre of studies with accent on freedom and hauteur = high risk.

6   'Aufidius Bassus contd, I–XXXI.' [*No comment*]

'*Natural History. I–XXXVII.*'
= *diffuse/scholarly work; no less variety than actual Nature.*

7   Wondrous, you find: all those books, and plenty in them so gritty, brought to release by a busy bee? You'll wonder all the more if you learn that for a considerable stretch of time he actively conducted law cases, passed away in his fifty-sixth year, and spent his middle period of time spread thin and tied down (a) by top-notch duties, (b) by serving as friend to emperors.

8   But this was a sharp talent, study-driven beyond belief, 110 per cent awake. Midnight oil would start at the festival of Vulcan, not to take the auspices, but for instant study from dead of night, in winter in fact from hour 7 or at latest 8, frequently 6.

Someone sleep came to readily, not unheard of for it to drive in, and quit, right in the middle of studies.

9   Before daybreak, off to Emperor Vespasian (another habitual night-user); next, off to the by-appointment duty. On return home, what was left of time, studies collected as their due . . .

10 After food (taken in the day light-'n'-easy, Olden Days style), often in summer if off work he'd lie in the sun, have a book read, with him taking notes and extracts: he read nothing he didn't do for extracts – and, he'd say, no book existed so bad that somewhere in it wasn't usable.

11 After sun, usually bathed in cold water; then a bite and tiny sleep; right away, as if making an extra day, study > time for dinner. Over which, book-reading/note-taking, yes, at a gallop.

12 I remember one of his friends pulled up the reader when he'd mispronounced something, and had it repeated: my uncle said to him, 'You did understand?' When he nodded, 'So why pull him up? We've lost ten verses plus through you interrupting'. Now that is what can only be called the 'Time Scrooge'.

13 Up in summer from table in daylight, in winter inside hour 1, as though some law dictated it.

14 This in the middle of one effort after another, the hurly-burly of Rome. Away from the city, only bathtime = study depriva-tion (and when I say 'bath', I'm talking about the core of the baths. You see, during rub-down and towelling, he listened to something or dictated).

15 For travel, as if freed from other cares, he was available for just one – namely, a shorthand p. a. by his side, plus book and note-books, hands protected with mittens in winter so not even harsh weather should snatch away any study time at all. That is why he travelled round Rome, too, by sedan-chair.

16 I recall myself being reprimanded by him – why walk?: 'You had the chance', he said, 'to waste not these hours'. You see, he reckoned all time 'wasted' which was not invested in study.

17 This heave got all those books out; it also bequeathed to me:

> 'Draft Copy with *Auszüge* (Vols 1–160*)'. Double-sided.
> Written in minuscule hand.
> [* Multiply this figure to take account of the data.]

His own story was, he could have sold these *Drafts* during his administration in Spain* for 400,000 sesterces, to Larcius Licinus.

[* At that stage, the numbers were considerably lower.]

18 Don't you (a) find yourself reflecting on how much he read, how much he wrote, and he doesn't seem to have been engaged in any duties at all/in the emperor's friend role, but, then again, when you (b) hear what effort he invested in his studies, he doesn't seem to have written/read *enough*? For what is there that either (a) those busy demands would *not* tie down *impossibly* or (b) this non-stop drive would *possibly not* get done?

19 That's why I do have to laugh when people call me 'studious student', when if I'm to be compared to him, I'm 'top at sitting back'. Me . . . as much as *him*? – when I'm torn everywhichway by duties of (i) state + (ii) friends? Who is there in that lot whose whole lives = sitting down with literature, in comparison with him, wouldn't blush red, sort-of surrendered to sleep and sloth?

20 An extended letter from me, when I *had* determined to write only what you ask for. Still. I am confident that all this will bring no less pleasure than the actual books: it has the potential to get you not only to read them but also to work up some similar effort – to stir you up with every stimulus of competitiveness. Farewell.

This is a time and motion study, it runs through Pliny's motions, promotions, and emotions, showing how he lived to read and write. How he 'read' reading and writing, and now we must try to 'read' him. How he read 'life' as a challenge to find time to read and write, *and* to live. How he did it his way. Yes, his books are a 'Natural History' *of Pliny*. They are his life – every time, a quart from a pint pot.

We can take *full* measure of the 'facts, facts, facts' fanaticism of this hunger-artist straight from the horse's mouth – 'You will have for proof of this passion of mine the fact that I have prefaced these volumes with the author names of the sources' – by sampling the relevant portion of Book 1's new information technology, the 'table of contents, book by book':

Pliny, *Natural History* I: Index for Book 19
Contents:

> **Flax**, nature and wonders of [= 19 §3]; 27 excellent vari-
> eties of; how sown [= 7] and processed [= 16]; when first
> coverings over theatre [= 23] . . . [etc., etc.] . . . The Garden:
> charm of [= 49]. Organization of items growing in the
> ground (apart from crops and shrubs. Nature + varieties +
> research: 20 items growing in the garden [= 60]. On all
> their roots, flowers, leafage. Which garden plants shed leaves
> [= 100]. How many days for each species to grow [= 117].
> Seed, nature of [= 119]. How each sows [= 121]. Which
> ones have a single variety [= 123], which have several [=
> 123]. Nature + varieties + research: 23 items sown in the
> garden to produce seasoning [= (160)]. Which items grow
> from a sap 'tear' [= 162]. **Fennel** family, 4 varieties [= 173].
> **Hemp** [= 173]. Diseases of garden plants [= 176]; reme-
> dies: ways to get **ants** killed [= 178]; remedies against
> **caterpillars** [= 180], against **gnats** [= 180]. Which ones
> salt water favours [= 182]. Method for irrigating the garden
> [= 183]. On the juice and flavour of garden plants [= 186].
> On **pepperwort, rosemary, *'zmyrnion'*** [= 187].

Grand Total:

> Items + research + remarks = 1,144.

Sources Excerpted:

> Maccius Plautus, Marcus **Varro**, Decimus Silanus, **Cato** the
> Censor, Hyginus, **Virgil**, Mucianus, Celsus, **Columella**,
> Calpurnius Bassus, Mamilius Sura, Sabinus Tiro, Licinius
> Macer, Quintus Birrius, Vibius Rufinus, Caesennius, author
> of *Gardening*, Castritus, *ditto*, Firmus, *ditto*, Potitus, *ditto*.

Non-Roman Sources:

> Herodotus, Theophrastus, Democritus, Aristomachus,
> Menander, author of *Tips for Living*, Anaxilaus.

For the *Natural Histories* as a whole, they say, Pliny lists 473 sources, just
146 of them as Latin. *Gardening* seems to have drawn Roman writers in
their droves. You will find yourself recognizing that Pliny puts his outsize

heart into his long haul of 'data and don'ta' on seeds and plants, world-wide. Not specially, I think, because he huffs and puffs himself at the start into one of his earnest impersonations of the archetypal Roman voice of the censorious Cato – busily excoriating the decadence of imperial Rome as it became the ancient world's superpower in the Second Century BCE. (For Cato's jumbled *On Agriculture*, see Dalby (1998), Gratwick (2002) in *Further Reading: General*. One odd chapter there at the death, on setting in asparagus (146), does not a tract on gardening make.) In most respects, these tirades make for entertainingly uneven bursts of bustling energy with scarcely any attempt to achieve persuasion or perspective. They tie the omnivorously culled information to Rome, to now, to 'us', by pressing local, insider, colour onto the page. This helps to bat away any automaton feel to this omnium gatherum. Pliny himself would, however, be scandalized if we failed to see that he was in these pages being the Roman Theophrastus.

This great pupil and successor of Aristotle produced reams of theory-driven treatises, among them a pair of systematic taxonomies of plant forms (see Date chart). Much of the information recycled by Pliny was excerpted from these, most probably directly, and for once we have a quality-check on the *Natural History*. I'm afraid Pliny's research reputation comes out of this bruised and battered – black and blue, in fact (see notes on Chapter 3).

Nevertheless, zest prevails. Pliny's keen eye for the quirky insert keeps relieving, and unsettling, his delivery of systematic typology. His drive to get those facts – all of 'em – suits gardening multi-culture just fine. He has more to say about each kitchen vegetable, each herbal organic salve, than anyone. Matching Greek science with Roman, Italian, empire market lore and produce distribution for all he is worth. And indulging the incorrigible gardener's hunger for sorting and typing, naming and grouping, verifying and varying . . . Without losing any chance of tying oddity to species, whether pointing out the peculiarities of common or garden familiars, or propagating strange notions of exotic imports. Just the way any decent gardening book, programme or event *must*. The specialist and purist Columella would shudder, very likely, but *Natural History* 19 is an indispensable part of the *Roman Book of Gardening*.

VI

Last in line, we saw, comes **Palladius**. His brainwave, to tie all the instructions for each plant to the entry on planting time, i.e. to its first mention in the calendar year, is pure good sense. All the same, any gardener can see that the plan is bound to foul up in the face of practice. Far too many plants sow in the same few months – and if they sow in autumn, most all of them already featured in spring as well. Gardening jobs *look* as though they bunch alarmingly; and the seasonal cycle of growing patterns does make this inescapable. But the allocation of time to gardening on the farm also tended to shove it into lulls between heavier demands – putting in grain, especially, and harvesting it. So the practical gardening manual must overload some entries, and starve others, even more than need be, in their own right. The best time to read one would be when there was too little that needed doing – and that would be when it would be both easiest to read and least worth reading! All gardening books are stuck this way. That's half the charm. Just like gardening.

Palladius' first book makes it pretty clear that the *World of the Countryside* is for appreciative *reading* as well as ad hoc consultation or ad rem use. Neat criteria for choosing a location are soon followed by a systematic review of the fabric of a farm – cisterns, stores, stables and yard, aviary, augmented by dovecotes, fowl, water basins, byre, and vegetable garden (at last!). After a few 'remedies', the picture is filled out with threshing-floor, bee-hives, baths, water-proofing, watermill, and tools, listed along with protective clothing. There is nothing here about the workforce, managerial structure, or marketing. In short, Palladius' farm is filled out with all the facilities that become a wondrously perfect playground for hard-slogging *readers*. His 'go-do-it' teaching certainly did run real farming in early modern Europe; and the complete blanking out of all connection between the farm he envisages and any world beyond brings us up close as can be to the handling of soil and seed, plant and pest, where gardening comes alive most of all. He also wrote on veterinary medicine, and grafted a (surviving) 'poem' on grafting.

VII

Between them, these translations give you virtually all we have by way of Roman gardening, and though today they are utterly unread even by classicists, they were widely influential in Renaissance culture. (The ancient medicinal garden seeded the mediaeval 'cloister-garden'. You can visit the ninth century *Hortulus* – with one bed/paragraph each for 24 precious plants – set out in verse by Walahfrid Strabo, either as now brought back to life in a 1981 UNESCO programme at Lorsch in Saxony,

or as diagrammed for the planet at http://www.kloster-lorsch.de/kloster/
garten.html. This phytotherapeutic tradition grew into modern ethnob-
otany: see Storl (2001) in *Further Reading: General*.)

These gardeners have enough strange asides and incidental weirdness to
keep readers gasping (bat skull scares and menstruation phobia), but they
also have all the familiar heaving and chopping that gardeners recognize as
the stuff of gardening – water and manure, digging and hoeing, and (as
Columella very nearly says) weeding, weeding, weeding. Naturally, there
is no talk of 'chemicals' – bone meal and dried blood, phosphates and rota-
tion – and many of our favourite species aren't on board – tomato and
potato, capsicum, sweetcorn, aubergine. But Romans knew how much
there is to tell about cabbage and lettuce, what can be done with roots and
stems, leaves and florets. Yes, this knowledge was a significant part of the
Roman power system, the archive of technology that represented control
of the Mediterranean for an imperial culture. But there is something
importantly 'Roman', too, about respect for spade and sluice.

All our texts get right down into the beds and trenches with the
gardener, smearing dung on seeds, dangling cucumbers, shaking out caterpillars. They stay close to the soil, watering, digging over, manuring. They
teach techniques of planting, timing sequences, tuning into stars, weather,
local peculiarities, traditional practices and lore. They make for straight
gardener's reading material, familiar and live, for all the cultural differences. True, gardening isn't what it once was; but, then, it never is (or
was). For one thing, their plant-names were not ours (or Linnaeus'), nor
were their plants. And translation from Latin to English is bound to fudge
and falter at least as much as translation from Greek to Latin for the
Romans (See Preface n. 2, Chapter 1 n. 9, Chapter 2 nn 21, 22, 31, 33,
49, Chapters 3 nn 34, 47, 49, 60, 65, 70, 76, 79, 90, Chapter 4 n. 12).
None of *our* lives can depend or rely on our gardens for real – food for the
farmer's table, produce for market in the nearest town (Introduction,
Virgil, *Georgic* IV.133, Columella 11.3.1, 10. Preface, 137, 310, Pliny,
Natural History 19.52, 57). Quite contrary. All the same, so much of gardening is grounded in basic body skills, it's easy to feel in touch with all
the work to be done in the *hortus*. Even though no one then *pictured* the
likes of themselves doing the dirty work: tough ancestors had once dug
and sweated; a decent farm now ran on slave labour (see ills. 2, 6, 7, 8).

But do read on.

See how *The Roman Book of Gardening* grows – grows on you.

Plate 3 Paul Cézanne, Portrait of a Farmer, 1901–6. Oil on canvas, 65 × 54 cm (cat. no. 488).

INTRODUCTION
Virgil: Reserving a plot

VIRGIL, *GEORGIC FOUR* 116–48

Now my tasks approach their final goal, I stow away sail,
in haste to put in, and land. If I were not, believe me,
my verse might visit rich gardens to write – 'at Paestum **rose**
beds crop twice'[1] – all the glory of gardening: *how to care?*
120 How do **endives**[2] rejoice to drink down the runnels, while
banks go green with wild **celery**, and writhing through grass
cucumber grows itself a belly? Yes, late in leaf
narcissus I would include, pliant **acanthus**' stem,
pale blanching **ivy**, and **myrtle** hugging the shoreline.

125 On approach to Fort Oebal towers, my memory's of *me*,[3]
where black river Galaesus wets farmed fields' burnish of gold.
I saw a Corycian old-timer. He had just a few
acres of country set aside, no blessing for bullocks
in crop yield, no good for sheep, no potential for wine.

130 Yet here among **brambles** he pushed down deep well-spaced veg.,
white **lilies** in a ring, with **vervain**, and with frail **poppy**.
His spirits were worth a king's treasure, when he went home late
at night, and there piled on his table a feast that cost nowt.

First in spring to pick **roses**, and then **apples** in the fall.
135 Now the chill of grim winter was still shivering the rock,
the ice was still reining the waters' flow, and him out there

29

already to snip the overgrowth from soft **hyacinth**.
Cursing: 'Late sodding summer! West bloody winds which drag on!'

That is why his bees reproduced, so his swarm multiplied,
140 he was first to profusion, first to squeeze combs, and gather
the honey. He had **lindens** and the most oozing of **pines** –
every bud that each fruit tree put on at its early bloom,
every last one of them it kept to ripen through the fall.

Another thing he did was leave **elms** late to shift into lines.
145 Hardened the **pear** tree first. Had **blackthorn** already bear **plums**.
And the **plane** already serve shade for folks having a drink. –

– But, believe me, I'm barred from this: space is my enemy.
I must pass by, leave gardening books for Virgils to come.[4]

Plate 4 Statuette of Priapus from Herculaneum. First century BCE. Bronze. Museo
Archeoligo Nazionale di Napoli (inv. 27731).

1

FROM COLUMELLA *ELEVEN*

Produce in prose

(1) *Preface* (11.1.1–2)

Claudius, priest of imperial cult, is one of nature's gentlemen.[1]
Equally, the young man is highly cultured. Stimulated by
discussions with more than a few expert enthusiasts, particularly with farmers, he pounded me into agreeing to draw up a
systematic *Horticulture* in Latin prose. His success in this did
not indeed escape me when I was wrapping the aforesaid topic
in the code of poetic law.

But you, Woody Esq.,[2] were persistently requesting a taste of
my verse-writing, and I didn't manage to say no. If you felt like
me about it, I was at once going to do what I am presently
moving on to, a postscript on *How to Run a Farm: the Job of Farm
Manager*, attached by way of supplement: *Garden Care*.[3]

True, I felt I had already to a certain extent gone through this in
Columella, On the Countryside, Book One.[4] But my imperial priest
lobbied for it, over and over, and came on just as strong. So I have
overrun the tally of *Books* that I was just on the point of completing, and I now put into the public domain this *Manual of
Country Life: Eleven*.

(2) The chapter on gardens (11.3)

1   Now that we have reviewed the *Work Assignments of a Farm Manager*, what must get done, at their specific times through the year, I shall honour my promise and append a supplement: *On Horticulture*. Garden Care will be just as much of an obligation for the Farm Manager, objective (1) being to lighten the cost of feeding himself, while objective (2) is to offer the owner, any time he comes, what the Poet calls a country 'feast that cost nowt'.[5]

2   § In the book he entitled *The Georgics*, Democritus reckons that people who build **garden walls** are being shortsighted, since a stone wall made of brick can't last for ever, as it normally gets attacked by rain and storm, and on the other hand the outlay rules out stone, way over the top in terms of relative importance. 'Should anyone want to enclose a decent-size area, they need to come into a fortune.'[6] Very well, then, I shall point out a method which lets us wall off a garden, from trespass by people or livestock, *without* major input.

3   § The earliest authorities preferred a living **hedge** to anything built, because it not only wants smaller outlay, but also lasts much longer through measureless time. That's why they handed down the following method of making a thicket by sowing **thorns**.

4   Take the spot you have decided to hedge. Immediately after the autumn equinox, as soon as the ground is wet with rain, the perimeter must be trenched right round with two furrows three feet apart. Maximum depth of trench: two feet is plenty.

Now, though, we'll leave them empty through the winter, first **preparing seed** to sow them with. The seeds are those of the giant thorns, above all **bramble**, **Christ's thorn**, and the one the Greeks call '*kunosbatos*', and we call **Dog's Briar**.

5   These **bramble** seeds must pick as ripe as possible. Mix with milled vetch flour. A sprinkling of water, and it is smeared on old sea-going cables or else any other ropes you like. Then the lines are dried, and stored in the loft. Not for long. Once midwinter is

done, forty days intervene, then around when the swallow arrives and the west wind starts to get up, after the Ides of February,[7] any water that was settled in the furrows through the winter is drawn off, and the loose earth that was dug out in autumn is put back

6 to half the depth of the furrow. Fetch the aforesaid lines from the loft, and roll out. Stretch them lengthways along both furrows. Then bury them. Only, see that the thorn seed sticking to bulges in those lines is not heaped over with too much soil. They must be able to grow up through it. As a rule, they poke out before thirty days are out. Once they have started to develop a bit, they must be trained to lean in towards the available space in between the furrows.

7 A hedge of **twigs** will need setting to plug the gaps. The briars of both furrows can spread out over this, and it can be something they can rest on, from time to time, as a sort of **prop** until they are sturdy. This thicket obviously cannot be destroyed short of digging it up, roots and all. Otherwise, it's beyond a doubt, it grows back after fire damage, improved. And so this is the very method of garden enclosure that won most approval from people of old.

8 § **Choice of site** will work out, the lie of the land permitting, beside the villa. Preferably rich in **soil**, a site with the possibility of **irrigation**, whether from a stream abutting, or if there is no running water, from a well source. For a well to win credence for year round supply, it must be dug out at the precise moment when the sun occupies the last segment of Virgo, i.e. September before the autumn equinox. This on the basis that the resources of springs are most fully checked out when the soil lacks rain water, after the lengthy dry period of summer.

9 NB A **precaution**: a garden must not lie below a threshing-floor. The wind must be in no position to carry bits of chaff and dust to it, in the course of threshing. Both are no friends to veg.

§ Next topic: **preparation** and digging over of **soil**. There are **two seasons**, because there are **two sowings**. Most seeds are sown in both autumn and spring.

Better in **spring** for **well-watered spots**, since the new-born year's gentleness welcomes the emerging seeds. Also, summer thirst is doused by water from the spring.

10 But where the nature of the site allows **no water** to be fetched in by hand, nor on the other hand to be served up on its own account, there is no other recourse than **winter** rains.

All the same, even at the most drought-ridden spots, the work can be shepherded by **digging over** the ground extra deep. Digging out a three-foot fall is plenty (what was dug out raises
11 the overall depth to four). But where there is plenty of water for irrigation, it will be enough for the fallow land to be turned with a shallow trenching tool, i.e. a spade with a blade under two feet long. Now we shall take care that the land which must be sown in spring is turned over in autumn, around the first of November. Land we mean to start up in autumn, we shall turn in May. That way the clods will loosen through winter cold or else summer sun, and the grass roots will be killed.

We shall need to **muckspread** not much earlier: in fact, when sowing time draws near, four days to go, the site must be stripped of grass and spread with muck, then the digging gone
12 over again, so scrupulously that soil and shit blend. The best dung for this purpose is the ass's, because it breeds least grass. Second best are either cowflops, or sheep's heaps if soaked for a year. The stuff humans do may well be regarded as the finest of all, but all the same there is no need to put it to work – except for bare gravel, or for the very loosest grade sand, completely devoid of vigour, in which case, to be sure, more power-packed nutrition is wanted.

13 So then the soil which we marked down for spring sowing we shall after autumn dig up and let lie, for parching by midwinter cold and hoar frost. In a mirror process, the force of cold cooks the earth just like the heat of summer, and loosens it by fermentation.

So now that midwinter is quite over, at long last the slurry will be tipped on, and around the Ides of January the soil is dug a second time round and split into **beds**.

> NB The pattern of these, though, must ensure that the weeders' hands easily reach halfway across their width, so when they follow up weeds they won't have to tread on the seeds. Instead, they can walk along paths, and weed half beds turn and turn about.

14 § So far has all been things to get done before sowing: enough. Now for instructions on what needs **cultivating and/or seeding, season by season**.

§ First up for discussion are species which can be sown at **two seasons**, i.e. autumn and spring. These seeds are: **cabbages** and **lettuces**; **artichoke, rocket, cress, coriander, chervil, dill, parsnip, rampion, poppy**. Sowing around 1 September, or better in February before 1 March.

15 > NB On arid or warm spots, such as the coasts of Calabria and Apulia, they can be trusted to the earth around the Ides of January.

§ Going back to seeds due for sowing only in **autumn**, on the condition, that is, that we live in coastal or sunny country, they are pretty well as follows: **garlic, small-top onions, 'Punic garlic', mustard**.

§ But now let me switch to sorting on a **month by month** basis what is normally suited by which season for entrusting to earth:

16 > So now, after 1 **January**, get busy, peeler **pepperwort** will be right to set in.
>
> In **February, rue**, in either seedling or seed form, and **asparagus**; likewise **onion** seed and **leek** seed. Same goes, if you're after spring plus autumn cropping, you will bury seeds of **Syrian radish, turnip, navew. Garlic** and **Punic garlic** are the last setting of this season.

17 > Now around 1 **March, leek** can shift to a sunny spot, once it fills out big. Likewise **all-heal**, in the last bit of March.

Then around 1 **April**, same for **leek, elecampane,** the late-late variety of **rue**. Likewise, to get them to take earlier, sow **cucumber, gourd, caper. Beet** seed, now, is best sown just when Punic pomegranate is in bloom.

18 **Leek** top still puts up with being moved on around the Ides of **May**.

After that, nothing should be buried in the ground as **summer** approaches, except **parsley** seed. Provided you'll water it, though: that way, it comes on just perfect through the summer.

For the rest, in **August**, around Feast of Vulcan time,[8] there is the third sowing. That is best for **radish** and **turnip** seed, ditto **navew** and **rampion**, not to forget black **alexanders**.

19 § Such are the seasons for sowing. Now to tell of the **individual** species which want some special **care**.

NB Everything I leave aside will have to be understood as calling for no service except for the weeder's. Of the latter, this can be said once for all: at every moment in time, plan to get rid of **weeds**.

20 § The **garlic** that some call '**Punic**', but the Greeks name 'aphroskorodon', develops to a much greater size than **common garlic**. Around 1 October, before it is put in, it will split from one head into quite a few cloves. For it has, like garlic, quite a few clumped spikes, and when they are split, they should be sown on 'ridges', so that they are cushioned on a raised growing position and suffer less damage from all the water in winter.

21 The 'ridge' is like the 'bar' made by countryfolk in sowing their lands in order to avoid waterlogging. But the one in the garden has to be smaller scale, and along its highest bit, i.e. its back, there must be spaced and planted, at intervals of a palm's width, the spikes of Punic garlic – or of **common garlic**, which is also sown just this same way. The ridges' furrows must be half a foot apart. Then, once the spikes have put out three sheathing leaves, hoe them. The more often this is done, the larger the seeds can develop. Then, before they make a stalk, twisting all

the green showing above ground and flattening it onto the earth
will help enlarge giant crowns.

22   NB In regions which get hoar frost, neither of these two
should be sown through the autumn. They spoil, in
midwinter time – which generally gets milder in January.
And that is why at cold spots the best time for setting in
garlic, common or Punic, is around the Ides of the aforesaid
month. But whatever the time is when we're either sowing
them, or now they are ripe we're storing them in the loft,
we will keep it going that during those minutes when they
are being buried or lifted, the moon is always underground.
Planted like that, or again put away like that, they are
thought neither to turn out maximum sharp in flavour nor

23   to make the breath of those who chomp them stink. All
the same, many sow them before 1 January, at mid day in
December, warmth in the air and lie of the land permitting.

§ **Cabbage** should be moved on when it has six leaves. In such
a way that its root shall first be smeared in liquid dung, rolled
up in three strips of seaweed, and then pushed home. Doing
this ensures that in cooking it mushes more quickly, and keeps
its green colour without soda.

    NB In cold and rainy regions, its setting is best after the Ides

24   of April. When its pressed in seedlings have taken, so far
as the gardener's plan allows, cabbage that is hoed and
manured more often builds better, and gets stem and sprout
growth of fuller size. Some people set this same plant at
sunnier spots from 1 March. But the majority of them spurt
into sprout, and afterwards, when it has been cut one time,
it makes no decent winter stalk. Though you can shift on
even the largest stalks twice. If you do do that, they are said
to offer more seed and bigger growth.

25 § **Lettuce** should be shifted with the same number of leaves as
cabbage. In sunny and coastal spots, it is best set in autumn,
but with inland and cold sites it's the opposite: pushed out into
position in winter, it doesn't do so well. But the root of this
one too should be smeared with dung. It wants a greater supply
of water, and that way its leaves are more tender.

26   Now there are quite a number of types of lettuce. Each needs to be sown at the right season. The one that is a dark or purple colour, or even a green colour and curly, e.g. '**Caecilian**', is good to sow broadcast in January. '**Cappadocian**', the one that grows with pale, '**combed**', compact, leaf, in February. The **white** one with the curliest leaf of all, as in the province of Baetis in the

27   territory of the township of Cadiz, is good to push in during March. The one of the '**Cypriot**' variety, red blush on white, leaf smooth and most tender, is fine for setting out all the way up to the Ides of April. On the whole, though, given sunny atmospheric conditions and at spots with plenty of water, lettuce can be sown virtually the year round.

> NB To get it to form a stalk more slowly: once it has developed to some size, give it a little shard in its heart. Held down by this sort-of 'load', it spreads horizontal and wide. The same method belongs to the endive, as well, except that it is more winter tolerant. That is why it can be sown even in cold regions at the start of autumn.

28   § Shoots of **artichoke** we'll do well to set out during the autumn equinox. Sowing the seed we'll fit in well around 1 March. And the seedlings we'll press in before 1 November, manuring with ashes galore. For that kind of manure seems to suit this veg. best.

29   § **Mustard** and **coriander**, not to mention **rocket** and **basil**, just as they were sown, they stay for good without being shifted from their position. They get no other cultivation than manuring and weeding. They can be sown not just in autumn but also in spring.

> NB Mustard seedlings shifted at the start of spring bring more sprout in winter.

§ **All-heal** is sown most thinly at both seasons in light well-worked soil, so it develops greater size.

> NB Spring sowing is better, though.

30   § If you fancy doing **chives**, earlier generations have instructed that it be sown pretty thick and then left alone; when it has grown that way, it is cut. But experience has taught us that it

gets much better if you leave space, and squash it down the same way you do a **leek**, at medium-sized intervals, i.e. no more than four inches. When it has become sturdy, cut it.

31   NB In the case of a leek that you want to make have a big head, it must be ensured that before you shift and plant it, you chop away all the minor roots and shear the top portion of the root fibrils. Then small shards or shells are buried beside them, a sort-of footing put under individual seeds, to make crowns of broader growth develop.

32   Cultivation of the **leek** is non-stop hoeing and manuring. No different is that of the **chive**, except that it must be watered, manured and hoed every single time it is cropped.

    NB Its seed in hot spots is sown in January: cold ones, February. To make it develop greater size, quite a few seeds are fastened in thin linen gauze and buried that way. On coming up in spots which cannot have water served up, it must be left space, around the autumn equinox. But where you can lay on moisture, it is right to shift it in May.

33   § For **celery**, you could use seedlings or sow seed.[9] But it is exceptionally glad of water, and for that reason is most handy planted beside a spring. Now if anyone wishes to make it broad-leaved, then as much seed as three fingers can get hold of should fasten in a bit of thin linen gauze, and that way it should be spaced out and deported to micro-beds. Or if it is preferred to grow curly-leaved, its seed should be stuck in a mortar, pound with a pestle of willow, buff up, and likewise fasten in linen

34   gauze, bury. It can also go curly short of this effort, and no matter how it is sown, if once it grows you check its development by turning a roller over it.

    NB Best sowing time: after the Ides of May all the way to the solstice. It wants it warm, you see.

§ Generally **basil** is also sown during these days. When its seed is sown, it is meticulously heeled in using beetle or roller. If you left the soil up in the air, you see, the seed usually spoils.

35 § **Parsnip, rampion,** and **elecampane** grow sturdy in a trenched and manured spot. To develop to greater size, essential to plant them at minimum density. **Elecampane** suits sowing at three-foot intervals, as it makes giant clumps, and has creeping roots, like the knot, or eye, of a reed. All these require no cultivation except weed-removal by hoeing.

> NB They will be most suited to planting in the first half of September, or second half of August.

36 § **Alexanders,** some Greeks call it *'petroselinon'* (rock parsley), quite a few of them call it *'smurnaion'* ('myrrhesque'), must be planted on a trenched spot, especially beside a stone wall. (1) It enjoys shade, (2) it grows sturdy in any sort of spot. When you've sown it once, if you don't remove the whole thing from the roots, but release every second shrub for seed, it lasts an age, and requires light cultivation, just hoeing.

> NB Sowing commences from the Feast of Vulcan,[10] runs right through to 1 September; in addition, in January.

37 § **Mint** wants acid-free soaking ground. Therefore, it's good planting in March next to a spring. If the seed happens to fail, it's possible to gather wood mint from the fallow, and plant them out top down. Doing that removes the wildness and leaves it domesticated.

38 § **Rue** sown as autumn seed must shift and thin in May, to sunny ground; ash to heap round it, and weeding till it is sturdy, so it isn't killed by grass, etc. The weeding will need gloved hands. If you don't cover up, life-threatening sores start up. If you have in ignorance weeded with bare hands, and itching and swelling have set in, grease them well with olive oil at once, and then periodically.

> NB A shrub of this one lasts quite a few years without harm – unless a woman during her period comes into contact with it, and that makes it shrivel up.

39 § **Thyme,** *'cunila'* savory from overseas, and **wild thyme,** as I noted in an earlier *Book,*[11] are sown, with enthusiasm, more by

people taking care of hives than by gardeners. But I think it's not out of place to have them in the garden too, as an ingredient in seasoning, since they fit some foodstuffs best of all. They want a spot neither rich nor manured, but sunny instead, given that their natural habitat is the very poorest soil, mainly in coastal regions.

40   NB These things are sown as seed or planted as seedlings around the spring equinox – and yet it's better to space out immature seedlings of **thyme**: when they have been pressed in turned-over soil, so they don't take hold slowly, a dry thyme shrub must be crushed, and once it is ground, on the day before you want to put it to work, treat it with water; then, after this has taken on its sap, it is poured on the shrubs
41   you planted until it toughens them just right. '*Cunila*' savory, by contrast, is too lively to need extra investment of care.

§ **Pepperwort**, when you have got it planted out before 1 March, you can chop like **chives**, only less frequently. For it won't be for cutting after 1 November, since it dies off once spoiled by the cold – though it will hold up as a biennial provided it has been energetically hoed and manured. At many sites it even prolongs its active life right through a decade.

42   § **Beet** is buried as seed when the Punic pomegranate is in bloom. As soon as it has five leaves, like **cabbage**, it is spaced out in summer if it's a well-watered spot, or if it is arid, it will need spacing in autumn just after the rains set in.

§ **Chervil**, likewise **orach**, which Greeks call '*andraphaxis*', must be buried around 1 October, but in a spot with no extreme cold. For if the region has cruel winters, the seeds must be broadcast after the Ides of February, and allowed to keep their position.

§ **Poppy** and **dill** have the same terms for sowing as chervil and '*andraphaxis*'.

43   § Seeds of **cultivated asparagus**, and the **wild** sort country folk call '*corruda*', are usually prepared biennially. When you've buried them at a rich well-manured spot after the Ides of

February, in such a way that you plant in individual little trenches as much seed as three fingers can hold, normally after forty days they intertwine with each other, and make a sort of 'solidarity'; these rootlets tied and linked like this are called by gardeners 'sponges'.

44 After twenty-four months these suit shifting to a spot that is sunny, well-doused and -manured. Furrows are made with a gap of one foot between them and no more than three-quarters of a foot in depth; into this the 'spongelets' are pressed down so as to germinate easily through the soil cover. But in dry spots, the seeds are for spacing out in the lowest levels of the furrows, so they stay put, as if in tiny troughs; whereas in sodden spots, quite the opposite, the seed must be positioned in the spine of the ridge so they are not harmed by excess moisture.

45 At the start of the year, when they have been sown this way, the asparagus they have put out must be snapped off. If you wanted to pull it from the bottom while the rootlets are still tender and low strength, the whole 'spongelet' would come away. In the remaining years it must not be culled but pulled by the roots. Unless this is done, snapped stems hurt the 'eyes' of the 'sponges', so to speak putting them out, and won't allow them to put out **asparagus**. But the stem that grows last of all in the autumn season must not be completely removed: a section of it is to release for seed.

46 Next, when it has made a spike and the seed selection is done, the clustered stems left behind, just the way they are, must be burned in position, and then all the furrows get a good hoeing, and weeds a clearing; at once a dressing of dung or ash needs putting on, so all winter long its juice soaks with the rain to reach right to the root.

Then in spring before growing commences, the earth is for shifting with 'roebucks' – a type of two-pronged tool – so the stem can shoot up more easily, and thanks to the loosening of the soil the root gain fuller thickness.

47 § **Radish** root is good to sow twice in the year, once in February when we look forward to a spring crop, and then in August

around the Feast of Vulcan,[12] the late one. The second, though, is thought to be better, no doubt about it. Care for radish consists in burying in soil manured and dug; later when it has developed to some size, it should be heaped round periodically. For if it comes out above ground, it will go hard and pitted.

48 § **Cucumber** and **gourd**, when there is plenty of water, want rather little care: they are really bucked up by moisture.

But if they had to be sown in a dry spot, where it's not on to lay on irrigation, a ditch one and a half feet deep needs digging in February. Then after the Ides of March, say a third of the depth of the furrow needs masking with an inlay of straw, then immediate heaping with manured soil half way up the furrow, and after the seeds are set in water needs continual application until they grow; when they start to grow sturdy, their developing growth must be closely matched with additional soil until the furrow comes up to ground level. Cultivated this way the seed will do well enough without irrigation all summer long, and bring fruit of nicer flavour than irrigated ones do.

49 NB In well-watered spots, seed planting time is at the earliest possible time, though not before 1 March, so it can be shifted when the equinox is done.

Thou shalt plant top down the seed which comes from the mid point on the cucumber, so it develops to giant size. For they are perfectly adequate for use as containers, like Alexandrian **gourds**, once they dry.

50 But if you are aiming them at the food-market, seed taken from the neck of the cucumber will need sowing topside up, so its fruit will grow to a greater length, with more taper: then, for sure, it finds a bigger price than the rest.

NB A precaution, now: as far as possible at the spot where **cucumbers** or **gourds** are sown, there should be no admission at all for any woman. For generally contact with one emasculates the growth of sturdy specimens. And if she's having her period, just her look will kill immature young ones.

51 **Cucumber** goes tender and nicest if before you sow you soak its seed in milk. Some people, to make it turn out still tastier, do the same, only with honeyed wine.

But anyone wanting to have an early cucumber crop must fetch manured soil put in crates, once midwinter is done, and supply a moderate amount of water. Next, when the seeds have grown up, on warm days without sun set them out in the open, near a building so they have protection from any gusting. But in cold and storm, bring them in under cover – and keep doing this till the spring equinox is done. After that lower the crates whole into the ground. This way, this someone will have an early-ripening crop.

52 There is the further possibility, if it is worth the effort, of sticking wheels under really big containers, so they can be taken out and brought back inside again with reduced effort. Nonetheless, they will need to be masked with see-through sheets, so that even in the cold, on clear days, they can be taken
53 out safe for the sun. By this method, cucumber was delivered to the Emperor Tiberius[13] pretty well the year round.

> NB This, mind, can be done with lighter input, so I read in the native Egyptian Bolus of Mendes,[14] who instructs us to get **fennels** and **brambles** sown in the garden at a sunny, manured spot, in alternating rows. Then once the equinox is done cut them just slightly below the ground, use a wooden stem to loosen the **bramble** or **fennel** core, and insert dung; with the same technique implant **cucumber** seeds so that, for cure, in their growth they can join with the **brambles** and **fennels**. This way they are fed not by their own but by their surrogate mother root. And the graft's stock delivers **cucumber** fruit even in the cold.

This seed's second sowing is normally honoured at the Quinquatria festival.[15]

54 § **Caper** in very many provinces grows on fallow of its own accord.

But at sites where there is a lack of it, if it's for sowing it will want a dry spot. So it will need a little ditch put round it first, to

be filled with stone and lumps of lime or Punic clay, so there is some sort of armour-plating to stop the shrubs of the aforesaid seed being able to break through it – they usually go on the loose through the whole field, unless prevented by some physical
55 enclosure. This, mind, is not so much of a nuisance (they can be rooted out periodically), as their carrying virulent poison, and making soil barren with their sap.

For cultivation, it is happy with none or the very lightest – this is after all something that grows sturdy in abandoned fields without input from any countryfolk.

NB Sowing: at both equinoxes.

56 § The **onion** bed demands earth that has been dug often rather than turned more deeply. So the soil must be broken up from 1 November and on, so as to crumble in winter cold and hoary rime; after a forty-day gap, it's time for a follow-up repeat; leave a twenty-one-day interval, and then triplicate, plus immediate manuring. At once fork it level, the same all over, and plant out into beds, now all roots are destroyed.

57 Next, towards 1 February it is good to broadcast seed on a clear day. An amount of **savory** seed will mix in so we can have that, too. For it is nice to eat green, and if dried it is not without its use for seasoning garnishes. But the onion bed, now, is hoed even more regularly and certainly not less than four times over. If you want to extract seed, do set out in February the largest heads of the '**Ascalonian**' shallot, which is the best, at four- or five-inch gaps.

And when they start to grow green, do hoe no less than thrice.

58 Next they make a stalk, and do take best care of the stems' stiffness by positioning sort-of 'trellisettes' in between. You see, unless you set close-packed reeds out crosswise, rather like a latticed vine-arbour, the green onion stems will be flattened by the wind, and all of the seed will shake off. And, for sure, the selection mustn't take place before ripening starts, and a black hue arrives. Still, drying through must not be allowed, either,

47

or it all drops off. Instead, the green stems are for pulling off, to be sun-dried.

59 § **Navew** and **turnip** have two sowing times, and the same cultivation as **radish**, though the sowing in August is the better. A *iugerum* of land demands four *sextarii* of their seed, but in such a way that it is joined by just over a *hemina* of **Syrian radish** over and above this measure.

60 NB Anyone sowing these in summer, beware the ground-flea may through prolonged drought eat up the still tender leaves as they unfurl. To avoid this, the dust found over a vault or even the soot which sticks to ceilings over the hearth must be collected, and then, on the day before sowing takes place, it must be mixed up with seed, and water sprayed on to draw off the juice all the night long. Soaked like this,

61 next day they will be good to sow in place. Certain ancient authorities, such as Democritus,[16] instruct us to treat all seeds with the juice of the herb called **sedum**, and to use the same thing to fight back against minute creatures – which experience has taught us is indeed true. Nevertheless, because availability of this herb is not plentiful, we more frequently use soot and dust, as above, and with them take care of the plants' well-being suitably enough.

62 § **Turnip** seed, Hyginus thinks,[17] must be broadcast after threshing over the chaff that has fallen on the threshing-floor, because the heads get a boost from the soil's underlying hardness preventing them going down deep. I have tried this out several times in vain, so I reckon that it is better buried in well-dug soil like **radish** and **navew**.

NB Farmers specially scrupulous over the pieties to this day keep up the custom of praying as they sow these plants, 'may they grow for us, and also for our neighbours'.

63 In cold spots, where there is a fear of an autumn sowing being scorched by the winter rime, low trellises are made from reeds and poles, straw is chucked over the poles, and that way the seeds are defended from hoar frost.

In sunny regions, though, after rain the harmful creatures which are called 'rocket' caterpillars by us, but in Greek are named '*kampai*', invade. Either they must be picked off by hand or the vegetable clumps must be given a shake early each morning. This way, while they are still sluggish from the chill of night, once they drop off, they don't crawl up to the upper parts any

64   more. Yet doing this is redundant if before sowing the seeds soaked in the juice of the herb **sedum**, as I said above. The caterpillars do no harm to seeds treated this way.

> NB Democritus, however, in the book entitled in Greek *Peri Antipathon*,[18] maintains that these very minibeasts are killed off if a woman who is having her period walks thrice around each bed, with hair loose and feet bared: after that, all the little worms drop off, and so die.

65   § At this point end the instructions which are in my opinion needed on *Garden Care* and the *Duties of a Farm Manager*. He should, as I argued in the first part of this exposition, be educated and knowledgeable in every rural task. But it very often turns out that recall of what we have learned lets us down and it needs refreshing pretty regularly from the manual.

I have therefore added an appendix containing the *Topics of All Columella's Books*. As and when the need arises, finding what to look for in each book, and how to deal with each problem, will easily be possible.[19]

Plate 5 Details of a flower panel set in the ceiling of a room off the east side of the open courtyard of a house at Pompeii (I. Vi. 11).

2

COLUMELLA *TEN*

Flowery verse

WORLD OF THE COUNTRYSIDE: BOOK 10

(1) *Preface*

1   Your interest, Woody.[1] I pledged it you when you did the contract. Now be in full receipt of the outstanding wee dollop of payment. For in my nine books to date I have paid my due, *minus* this fraction: I do now pay up in full.

So, now, the negative balance outstanding is *horticulture*. Low energy and neglected by the ancient farmers of old. Today up there with even the most densely visited sites.

The reasons for this? Among people long ago, resource management used to mean more thrift. But those on low incomes actually had more lavish dining practices. Why? Because milk supplies, and meat from game and domestic animals, like water and corn, allowed tolerable diets for the highest and for the

2   lowest. In time, succeeding generations, above all our own, fixed feasts at depraved prices. Dinners are now rated in terms not of natural needs but of property ratings. Low-budget masses are herded away from high-price foodstuff and driven to down-

3   market food. That is why *Garden Care*, since produce has an increased role in current practices, must be more carefully prescribed by us than our ancestors handed it down.

Horticulture would now be subjoined to the earlier projects in prose delivery, the way I had planned, if my project had not been taken by storm by your insistent demands. Demands which prescribed that I must fill up in metrical verse the missing fraction of the *Georgics*, which Virgil, mind, **Virgil** himself, signalled he was 'leaving for gardening books' from authors 'to come'.[2]

4   No other way could I ever dare any such thing. Only in line with the wishes of the poet adored above all others. His godlike decree stirred me on. Without doubt I went stubbornly because of the difficulty of the work. But not without hope of a successful outcome. I have set about a subject which is meagre to a degree, virtually deprived of bulk. It is so spare that it could count as a sub-percentage of my task in the total aggregate of the whole work. In its own right, bounded by its own set of goals, it could no way have visible impact. For although it has many limbs, about which we can hold forth, nevertheless they are so minuscule that, in the Greek phrase, 'a rope of sand couldn't be wound' from their ungraspable microscale.[3]

5   So it is that this stuff – whatever came of my work through the night – claims no credit for itself. So much so, it counts it all to the good if it does not dishonour the legacy of earlier texts preserved as the publications of **Columella**.

     – But now I must end these disclaimers, my *Preface*.

(2) The poem

The garden

Add gardening culture. I'll teach you, Woody,[4]
all the data that once, when 'barred by space' his 'enemy',
when his verse was visiting 'joyful crops', 'Bacchus' gifts,
'you', too, 'great goddess Pales', and add 'heavenly honey',
5   Virgil 'left' for 'gardening books from' us 'Virgils to come'.[5]

First move. **A home** for a garden symphony, courtesy
of **rich soil** in the field.
                Crumbling clods and sloppy ridges
are sported. Dig, and it's a fair copy of fine grade sand.
The physics, the soil structure, is handy – happy grasses

10   are teeming, any wet makes **elder** grow those red berries.
As you see, dry soil gets thumbs down. Just like marsh flooded soil,
that suffers whingeing from frog, with its chorus eternal.[6]

Next, the soil that of its own accord rears up leafy **elms**,
wild vine joyful. **Wild pear** woods rough. Submerged by **plum**'s
   stoned fruit,
15   it exults. A carpet of **apple**'s volunteered plenty.
Yet refuses **hellebores**, including the white poison sap sort,
and suffers no **yews**, sweats no virulent toxins,
even when it has delivered the crazed 'half a human' plant
20   and produces the **mandrake** flowers. And the gloom of **hemlock**.
Both **fennel** canes (rough on hands) and (legs' enemy) **bramble**'s
face to the world. Let the soil grow **Christ's thorn** with spines so sharp.[7]

Note, **rivers** do make good neighbours. A toughened occupant
can fetch them to save a garden from its eternal thirst.
25   Or see that a **spring** weeps in a cistern bed none too deep.
In case dead weight tears hernias when they heave water up.

That is the right ground. Either use **walls** or else **thicket hedge**
to make an enclosure, and no way through for herd or thief.

Don't you shop for a masterpiece: 'handcraft of Daedalus'.
30   'By Polyclitus'. 'One of Phradmon's.' 'Or Ageladas'.'[8]
No art work, please. Take a trunk chipped into accidental shape.
An old tree to worship as the godhead of **Priapus**.
Phallic fright. Eternal presence. A garden's focal point.
Groin to menace the boy, the burglar shooed by his sickle.

35   Now let's go. 'Cultivation', calendar **times for sowing**
seeds, 'how to **care**' for the seedlings. 'Which star governs' the first
germination of flowers, 'rosebeds at Paestum' in bud;[9]
which governs 'Bacchus' stock'; the loading on surrogate stems
that bows down the mellow tree with the fruit she has fostered.
40   Pierian sisters, channel the song fine. Columella's Muses.[10]

Thirsty dog Sirius has now lapped down Ocean's waters.[11]
Titan Sun has now balanced his disc with equinox hours.
Autumn is brimming. He tosses his forehead, cider-stained
and soaked in fermenting juice. He tramps out the foaming grapes.

45 It's time that ironclad oak, my long-handled **spade**, got turning
acid-free ground: *if* all the rain has now tired and soaked it.
But if it stays coarse, just as it hardened when the sky stayed clear,
then command **streams** go on their way here down sloping runnels
so the earth can drink from the source, and fill full yawning mouths.

50 Now if moisture is not available, whether from sky, or from plain,
if the spot's character, or Jupiter, refuses rain,
wait for **winter**. Wait till Bacchus' Cnossian firecracker[12]
from cosmos' pinnacle is veiled by ocean's blue surface.
Till Atlas' girls fear the rising Sun squared up to face them.

55 Now his time comes: trust runs out in Olympus' defences.
Sungod Phoebus panics. Bolts from Scorpio's claws, those stings
from hell. Full speed on centaur Sagittarius' horseback.[13]
Rabble with no clue of your birth, don't spare your 'mother' – she's
fake.[14] One womb delivered the clay that Prometheus would mould.

60 The other was the parent who bore us. Back when storming
Neptune flooded the earth with the sea, right down in the deep
made the abyss quake, and terrorized river Lethe's waves.
A one-off, the time when all Hell saw the King of Styx quail.
Oceans in overload made waves among mutinous dead.

65 A teeming *hand* it took, on a planet lacking humans,
to create us. On that day boulders torn from mountains high
gave us birth, stones of Deucalion. –
                                        Whoa, hey, lazybones,
beat off that torpor this instant.[15] Use the ploughshare's curved teeth,

70 tear the greenery 'hair', now rip the 'weeds' she is wearing.
With heavyweight **rake**, score furrows into her wincing back.
With wide **mattock** scrape her womb, dig the bowels of the earth.
Don't stop to think. Mix the bits with the top inch of turf while
they're warm.[16] Set, and there let them lie for hoar frosts to scorch
      white.

75 At the mercy of Caurus, sub-zero lashings of sadism.
For wild Boreas to chain up, then Eurus can undo her.[17]

The year moves on. Midwinter from Riphaea's bleak and numb:
then it's Zephyr and defrost time.[18] Sunshine breeze, and sparkle.
The interstellar axis will lose Lyre, drowned in the deep,[19]
80   'Spring's on its way!' Prophecy will come from swallow's nest.[20]
Then a fattening cake is the thing: ass **dung**, say, in lumps,
or cowpat. Feed the ravenous earth till it wants no more.
The gardener *does it himself*. Basket straps snap with the load.
Get your fresh-ploughed fallow fed. There is no call for shame.
85   All the sewage toilets spew out, from the pipelines of filth.

Now rain compacted it, the top was hardened by ground frost.
Back to 'acid free ground': let **dibble** blade hack the surface.
Next they must give the turf's living growth, and the clods, a real
good bashing. Use the **rake**'s teeth (or even a cleft **mattock**'s).
90   Release that crumbly cornucopia: the fields are ready.

Work this in now. Grab a **hoe**. Hoes gleam through wear on the soil.
Engineer small-gauge channels. One end straight to the other.
Then go back, make a grid. Wee **paths** set at a right angle.

Attention. Now the earth has been combed, and the 'partings' are clear.
95   She stripped off soiled clothes, and she shines. Demands **seed** of her
      own.
Now. In all hues, paint the **flowers** – they are earth's own stars:
Snowdrops in shimmering white.[21] Burnished **marigold**-en eyes.
Sprays of **narcissus**. **Wild lion**'s raging mouth gaping wide
miming snap dragon.[22] **Lilies** putting their strength in white cups.
100 Lest we forget: **hyacinths** range from snow-white, to sky-blue.

Now. One pales down on the ground, one purples her leaves with gold,
both **violas**, and planting calls. Add **rose**, in overfull blush.

At this time, '**all-heal**', and its curative drops; the sap salve
of **celandine**; **poppies** to halter runaway sleep –
105 broadcast the lot. What puts an edge on men – 'arms' them for girls?
High-yield **onion** seed wanted. Ship it in from Megara,
and from Sicca, dug up through Gaetulian clods, and cropped.[23]
And from sowing next door to fertility god Priapus,

aphrodisiac **rocket** can rouse slacker husbands for sex.[24]
110 Wanted, dwarf **chervil**, and a lethargic palate's tonic,
 chicory. Wanted, sprouting **lettuce** with soft outer leaves,
 common garlic's crevassed heads, and smelling way off, the **Punic**
 sort – all the stuff handy for a working man's bean mix lunch.
 Wanted, **rampion**, and **radish**, rooted from Assyrian seed,
115 then chopped and diced, teamed up with soaked **lupines**, and served,
 to make you want mug after mug of good Pelusian beer.[25]
 Now or never, as well, for all those low-cost pickling plants,
 caper, bitter **elecampane**, and menacing **fennel**:
 get 'em in.
 Just as pressing: **mint**, how it spreads as it grows,
120 and **dill**, all those lovely perfumed blooms, have to be spaced out.
 Rue, too. Which will bring out full 'Athena berry' flavour.[26]
 Mustard. Which will bring tears to the eyes, provoked as and when.
 Plus drab **alexanders** and **onion** that makes you cry: roots
 for setting. **Pepperwort**'s the one to spice up milk to drink,
125 it'll wipe the tattoo sign, you bet, from a runaway's brow –
 which is why its Greek name 'peeler' says just what it can do.[27]

 Share the moment, heavy sow the most prevalent of plants[28] –
 thrives anywhere on Earth, for pauper, for arrogant king:
 it puts on their table stalks in winter, then shoots in spring.
130 Produce of historic Cumae, where slime carpets the shore;[29]
 of Marrucine Abruzzi; of Signia on Mount Lepine,
 ditto, rich-tilth of Capua, gardens at Caudine Forks,
 the famous Stabiae springs, Vesuvius' own countryside,
 'Parthenope', city of culture, 'dewed by Sebethos' rill';
135 of swamp and salt-pits next door (to you, sweet Pompeii and
 Herculaneum), where crystal clear River Siler flows down;
 of tough-guy Sabellians, who market multi-sprouting stock,
 same for Turnus' lake and orchard-town Tivoli fields, both;
 of Bruttium's soil, and 'mother, Aricia', of the **leek**.

140 Once we have committed seeds to earth after her release,
 she conceives and we see she gets non-stop cultivation and loving **care**,
 so our harvest will come in with returns plus interest piled high.
 My first commandment: bring in spring **water**, plenty of it.

Never let thirst scorch her baby once the seed has taken.
145 When she is at term, releases her strings, and opens up,
when the flower progeny shoots up from mother earth's field,
it's time to give the plant creche a moderate dousing, so
be the careful gardener when you water, when you comb
with your **fork** of steel, when you rid furrows of **weeds** that choke.
150 But if the garden sits on hillside grown over with bush,
and no stream ebbs down from the wood at the top of the rise,
then a **bank** must be built up from heaped clods, to make the patch
stand proud, and the plant can get used to living in dry dust.
Planted on elsewhere, it won't thirst, and be shocked at the heat.

155 In no time, ferry to cloud-born Phrixus, but not Helle,
emperor of stars and of flocks, will lift head above waves.[30]
Madonna earth will now spread bosom wide. Demand the seed,
surely full-grown, long to wed the plants put in her charge.
Men, be on your guard. It makes no sound when the seasons tread,
160 and bolt. No noise from the year as it turns on its axis.
Just look! Mother so mild is out protesting for her brood,
she both wants the babies she bore, and she wants them right now,
and she asks for her step-children, too. See ma has her kids,
the hour is come. They pledge her love, so crown matron in green
165 progeny: you garland her hair and you sort out her locks.
Now green **parsley** shall give flowery earth a fringe of curls.
Now **leek** shall let down long tresses, and in the release she
shall find joy, and **parsnip**[31] shall shade over her soft cleavage.
Now, the boon of a faraway plant's exotic perfume,
170 **saffron** Hybla must come down from the mountains of Sicily.[32]
Marjoram must at once arrive from festive Canopus.
Understudy of your tears, Cinyras' virgin daughter,
but myrrh drops' better, get set, Achaea's **sweet cicely**.
Those flowers that take rise from sadness, blood, a falsely
175 condemned – Ajax's flowers, and never-fading **amaranths**.
All the myriad hues that ritzy Nature delivers,
a mosaic in plants, by the gardener who sowed them as seeds.

Now come '*coramble*' cabbage – but (NB) this will harm eyes.[33]
Hurry at once, do fetch the **lettuce**.[34] Good health in the juice.
180 Relieves depressive eating problems, in chronic disease.
One sort grows green as it is dense; the other's dark hair shines,
of the **two varieties** named for **Caecilius** Metellus.
As type three, the **pale** lettuce with a packed but nice clean head,
keeps alive in its surname the stock of **Cappadocia**.
185 And there is mine, grown by **Cadiz** upon Tartessus' shore:
its wavy parting is bright white, bright **white** too is its stem.
Ditto, one that **Cyprus** rears, at Paphos, in the rich fields:
well-combed **purple** tresses, but stock is the colour of milk.

So many exhibits! Specified sowing times to match.[35]
190 First in the year, Aquarius sets the 'Caecilian' sort.
In the month of the dead, Pan presses in 'Cappadocian'.
On your month's first day, Mars, bed down the one from Tartessus.
On your month's first day, now, Venus, the one from your Paphos.

While the thing wants, looks to mate with, the mother who wants it,
195 and while that mother, so soft, lies there beneath giving ground,
germinate in her. Now is the cosmic mating season.
Now love spurts for intercourse. Now the spirit of the world
goes pell mell, raving for sex. Whipped then by lashings of lust
it falls in love with its children, fills them with pregnancies.
200 Now ocean's father, and now the sovereign of all water,
seduce one his Tethys, the other his Amphitrite.[36]
Now upon delivering a sea-god husband offspring,
both wives can show them off, fill the deep with creatures that swim.
Almighty god himself now drops his thunderbolt, the cad,
205 and reruns that classic fling with Acrisius' daughter.
He pours into mother's womb, in one brute of a downpour.
Mamma, she does not reject love from her loving son now,
but allows the coupling, inflamed with desire: Mother Earth.
So the seas, so the mountains, so the whole goddam cosmos
210 does the rites of spring. So humans', beasts' and birds' own desire.
Thus love ignites in the psyche, goes wild in the marrow,
until Venus gets enough, impregnates fertile organs,
generates all manner of broods, eternally quickens
the world with fresh young. Then ne'er shall the aeon slump barren.

215 — But how . . . — Why have I let my horses fly the stratosphere
race unreined? My brash stampede, up the path to the sublime.[37]
Such a theme for the bard that Delphi's bay, grandly infused
with gods' power, shoved towards theorizing the real. Priest
in mystic nature's holy rites, in heavens' sealed covenants.
220 Goaded on past Cybele's celibate Mount Dindyma,
past Cithaeron, past the Nysa mountain range of Bacchus,
past its own Parnassus range, on past the Muse-friendly hush
of Pierian grove. He is roaring in Bacchic frenzy's voice,
'You, Delos' Paean; you Hosanna, Hosanna Paean'.
225 I — I am Calliope's. What I love is so light. Now
she calls my vagaries home. Bids me race round a dwarf track.
And so, by her side, get weaving poems from finespun thread.
Verse for a tree surgeon to sing (Muse conducts), while he works,
trussed up in the trees. For the gardener, in the garden green.

230 So come, on with the next. With dwarf gaps between each furrow,
see that **cress** is broadcast. Bane of the intestinal worms
that a sick stomach rears, from food it just cannot manage.
And **savory**, taste reminiscent of thyme, common or Cretan.
And **cucumber** and **gourd**. One yielding, one delicate, neck.
235 Get rough **artichoke** set in. Nice for Bacchus when boozing,
it must come, although no fun for Apollo when singing.
At times this lifts up in a tight ball of purple clusters,
at times grows with myrtle-green tresses, and droops at the neck.
Now it stays opened out, now it's pine-shaped, topped off in a
240 point. Now it's basket-like, and bristles with menacing spines.
The occasional pale one apes all the twists of **bearsfoot**.[38]

In no time at all now, the **Punic tree** gets dressed in blooms
of blood-red.[39] It mellows with crimson casing round the seed.
Sowing time for **dragon-root**. Now, infamous **coriander**.
245 Whereas **git** grows, **fennel flower**, liked by spindly **cummin**.
And **asparagus'** berry rears up among thorny fern.
And **hollyhock mallow**, that tracks the sun with head hanging down.
Plus the brash one that apes your vines, O Bacchus of Nysa,
but fears no **briars**. For rising from **brambles**, villainous
250 black **bryony** strangles **wild pear** and undaunted **alder**.

Then comes . . . a Greek name. Just like the letter next to the first
when fixed in wax, by the blade of a qualified teacher.
So too, in the rich ground, with a blow from an ironclad spike,
pushed down, in it goes. Green of leaf, white of stem. It's . . . **Beet**[a].

255 Oyez, oyez. Harvest looms upon perfumed **flowers**: now.
The radiant spring: now. The year's kaleidoscopic offspring
paint mother's brow, and the make-over gladdens her heart: now.
Phrygian **lotus** premieres bud . . . jewel . . . shining eyes: now.
Violet beds release to the world shut-eye . . . bud . . . winking gems.
260 **Snap-lion** yawns wide.[40] The chaos of an instinctive blush,
the wide-open look of a virgin: **rose** offers tribute
to heaven, tinctured with Sheba's incense, bouquet for shrines.

Time I invoked you, Acheloids, the Pegasids' chums,[41]
those dancing Dryads on Maenalus, calling Woodland Nymphs,
265 living in Amphrysus' grove, living in Thessaly's Tempe,
living on Cyllene's range, or Lycaeus' country shade,
or moist caves forever dewed with Castalia's droplets,
and living at Sicily's Halesus, out picking blooms,
back when the daughter of Ceres was engrossed in your dance,
270 on Enna's plain, as she snipped lilies in blossom, in spring.
Was raped, and in a trice was bride of the despot of Lethe,
setting miserable shades higher than stars, preferring Hell
to heaven, Hades above Jupiter, death above life.
In the underworld empire, she is boss: Queen Proserpine.
275 You nymphs, too. Drop the funeral gloom, at last, drop the dread.
Tread easy and willing. Plant tender feet. Come over here.
Deck your devotional baskets, with those tresses of Earth.
No one lies in wait for nymphs here. No variation on rape.
Chaste Faith is Columella's cult. And the Saints of my Home.
280 A universe full of fun, free of care, peals of laughter.
Full case of wine, meadows of happiness, parties full swing.

Now's the cool of the spring. Now is the year at its mildest.
While the Sun god is fresh, he presses us, lie down on grass,
it is fresh. The springs run off, trilling, through groundcover green.
285 Pure pleasure to drink. No longer ice, not yet steam in the sun.

By now, gardens are wreathed with the blooms of Dione's girl.[42]
By now, **rose** matures brighter than the purple of Sarra.
Less radiant the gleam on the face of Leto's Phoebe
when Boreas scuds clouds from the north. Less scintillating
290   Sirius ablaze, or red Fire-Star, or Evening Star's
shimmering face, when Dawn Star returns to rise in the East.
Less resplendent Thaumas' daughter, burnished with spangled bow,
than a garden's iridescence, pleased with the dazzling brood.

So get on: whether now sunbeams rise, at night's finale,
295   or when the Sun god dives horses in the ocean past Spain,
wherever **marjoram** puts up a screen of perfumed shade,
cull **narcissus'** tresses, and non-fruiting pomegranate's.
You, too, Naiad, stop 'Alexis scorning Corydon's wealth',
'lovely as Alex is, you are lovelier still',[43]
300   fetch **violets** in baskets. Tie up **balsam**, bunched together
with **black privet**. Use **cassia**, and tie clusters of **saffron**.
Then spray with neat wine from Bacchus: Bacchus' wine spices scent.
All you countryside folk, with your calloused thumbs used to nip
velvet flowers, now you must take the bullrush **trug**, woven
305   from wicker now gone grey, pile **hyacinths** in it, rust-red.
Now **roses** must bulge out the threads of rush twine. And the bag
must split, under the payload of inflammatious **marigolds**,
so Vertumnus' cup runneth over, flush spring marketeer.[44]
Tottering along, once he is sozzled, gallons of wine,
310   the waggoner's sack must cart tons of cash, back from the town.

But the harvest will turn gold with ripe ears of corn. Titan
Sun will lengthen the day under the two-in-one starsign.[45]
He will torch with his flames the claws of the crab from Lerna.
The moment to twin **garlic** with **onions**, Ceres' **poppy**
315   with **dill**. While they are fresh, deliver them in trussed bunches.
Sing the praises of Lady Luck in Latin, thick and fast,
on clearing the goods.[46] Joy. Off you dash, back to the garden.
You scattered **basil** through fallow you have furrowed and watered:
now you must press it in. Compact it. Use heavy rollers.
320   Don't let the heat of soil crumbled to dust scorch the seedlings.
Don't let that titch, ground-flea, creep in and attack with its bite.

Don't give predatory ant a chance to plunder the seeds.
It's not just that out there daring to chomp up the young leaves
are snail coiled up in its shell, and fluffy caterpillar.
325 No, time come, when **cabbage** gets fat, and goes yellow, on its
toughened stalk, when the core of **beet** swells, and turns pale, when the
gardener has not a care. It's great! Now the goods are full grown.
Now they're ripe. He looks to slip the cutter in underneath.
Wild Jupiter's sky spears down sheets of hard rain. Regular.
330 His hail dynamites the toil of the man-and-oxen team.
Rain dew washes in teeming, pox-spreading, waves. Regular.
From it, enemies of Bacchus' **vines** and grey **osier** beds
issue, airborne. All through the garden, 'rocket'-creepy crawls:
its path over the surface burns up the seeds with its bite.
335 Their heads lose their tresses, until, stripped bare, they are topped,
and lie lopped, and die eaten away by the rank poison.
The country folk need not put up with these freaks of nature.
The actual variety of experienced reality
points the afflicted to modern remedial techniques.
While hard research, and the school itself of trial by use,
340 pass it on to agrobusiness: how to soothe maddened winds,
how Etruscan rites avert a storm, using the sacred.[47]
Here is how to stop the blight of *rust*, from scorching green growth:
appeasement, with a pup's blood, still unweaned, and his entrails.
Here's how, they do tell, ass-head, Arcadian, flayed to the bone,
345 was nailed by Tages, Etruscan, to the countryside's edge.
To ward off Almighty Jupiter's lightning bolts, Tarchon
hedged his property with white bryony vines. Regular.
Here's how the son of Amythaon, taught most things by Chiron,
hung out birds of the night, pinned to a cross, and put a stop
350 to them sobbing their songs of death, on the roofs of buildings.
For the prevention of dread creatures cropping the new yield,
it has been found, sometimes it helps to treat seeds with a good
shake of Athena's rich olive dregs (no, do not add salt),
or all they can take of black ash (use domestic build-up).
355 It has, I add, helped to pour over plants the acid fluid
from **horehound**, and to smear with plenty of sap from **sedum**.
But in case no treatment can fend off the infestation,
then Dardanian techniques must come in.[48] A woman must plant

her bared feet, as her time comes, when a good heifer like her
360 must serve natural law, and blood flows to her shame, unclean –
but she must walk free, loose at the breast, loose hair for last
   rites –
as thrice she is led round the beds, and hedge, of the garden.
Her step beats the bounds in lustration. Stupendous to see!
Just as when a tree gets a good shake, and a cloud rains down
365 of shiny round **apples**, say, or **acorn**'s protective case.
Down on the ground roll torn bodies. Convulsed caterpillar.[49]
So hypnotic spells once drugged the dragon, till it dropped off.
Slid down from Phrixus' fleece, so all of Iolcos could see.[50]

But, it's time, the season to **chop** those early 'first-cut' stalks,
370 and tear off the stems that come from Tartessus and Paphos,[51]
and then belt the bundles all around with **parsley** and **chive**.
Time, erotic **rocket** comes erect in perfumed garden.
Time, oily **sorrel**, time, **thamnum** shrubs, grow stiff by themselves.
And **squill**. **Butcher's broom**, bushed to make a bristling hedge, is
   now
375 pushing on. And wild *'corruda'* stem, **asparagus**' twin.
Moisture-retaining **purslain** seals cover for thirsty rows.
The **eye bean** spoils things for the **orach**, by rearing up tall.
Here, hanging in an outhouse, or there, like some watersnake,
out in the summer sun, all through the cool shade of the grass,
380 there creeps . . . **cucumber**. And swollen **gourd**, come to term.
   Ready
to pop. These last are not uniform. So if you like them
longer, the sort that hang down from a thin peak to its head,
pick seed from the slight neck. But if you want a globular
body, the sort that starts to swell up so huge at the womb,
385 you'll pick seed from the belly half-way, and that will give fruit
to pot Narycus' pitch, or Attica's Hymettus honey.
A pitcher fine for water, or a flask for Bacchus' wine.[52]
Then, too, a **gourd** will teach kids how to swim in the river.

Whereas a bruised-looking **cucumber**, grown a pregnant womb
390 – hair-covered, and like the adder hidden in knotty grass,
lying with its belly curled, tight in never-ending coil –

63

is noxious. It will aggravate immoral summer's blights.
It stinks, does its juice. With seeds, yes great fat seeds, it is stuffed.
But the one down in that outhouse creeps towards water flow,
395 giving chase as it slips away, gets real thin through this love
– the white sort, more a-tremble than . . . a just farrowed sow's teat,
more creamy than . . . milk thickened, before tipping in the cheese-
      moulds.
This will taste sweet. Go orange, take up moisture on soaked ground.
One day, it will come to the rescue of ailing mortals.

400 When Erigone's dog, set a-blaze by Hyperion's heat,[53]
opens up **fruit** of the orchard, and piles with **mulberries**
the pure white basket awash with the blood red of the gore,
it's time. Premature **fig** must come down from twice-cropping tree.
Wax-tinged **plums**, Armenian **apricots**, Damascus **damsons**
405 pack boxes, the fruit which exotic Persia once used to
export. Myth says, spiked with Persia's traditional poisons.[54]
Today the risk of death with each purchase is minimal.
They advertise divine juice, and forget they were lethal.
For a bonus: carrying the name of the same people,
410 quick-ripening 'Persians' hustle diminutive **peaches**.
In season, they swim in juice, huge ones, the produce of Gaul.
In winter cold, the late-yielding ones come in from Asia.
Under Arcturus' malign star, the next tree delivers:[55]
'Livian', rival of 'Chalcidian'; 'Caunian' rival of 'Chian';
415 purple variety: 'Chelidonian'; fat kind: 'Mariscan';
the one whose seed has a rose tint for fun: 'Callistruthian';
the white 'Albiceratan' that preserves the name of blond wax;
the cloven one: 'Libyan'; one with rainbow skin: 'Lydian'. **Figs**.[56]

Slow-foot Vulcan's rites are duly done,[57] and it's a bonus
420 sowing-time. Cloud cover is fresh. Water hangs in the sky:
turnip. The world-famous produce of Nursia's open plain.[58]
And '**bunias**', the French turnip. Fetched from Amiternum fields.

– But Columella's **grapes** are now **ripe**. Fearful lobbying
by 'Hosanna' Bacchus.[59] Who tells us, horticulture is done.
425 We **close** the garden **gate**. We countryfolk heed your command.

So exultant we do harvest your blessings, sweet Bacchus.
Among rutting Satyrs. Among Pans half-human, half-goat.[60]
Our arms wave now. They droop when the wine gets stale, and goes off.
'You, the Maenalian! You, Bacchus! You the Lyaean! And you,
430 father, the Lenaean!' we hymn. Invite him into our home.
So the wine-tank ferments, filled with lakes of Falernian wine.
The vats will boil and bubble with rich new must. Overspill.

§ At this point, Woody,[61] ends my lecture on horticulture.
In accordance with instructions from the interstellar bard.
435 Vergilius Maro. Who first 'dared unbar the old sources'.
Who 'read his Ascraean poem through all the towns of Rome'.[62]

Plate 6 Detail of plate 7, the Rustic Calendar mosaic at Saint-Romain-en-Gal. Musée des Antiquités nationales, Saint-Germain-en-Laye, Paris.

3

PLINY'S ENCYCLOPAEDIA

Nature's miracles

NATURAL HISTORY: BOOK 19

(1) From *Preface* (19.1–2)

1   The stellar and meteorological system has just been set out, ready for even novices to get, with no place left for doubt.[1] Those who truly understand find the countryside contributes no less to grasping the sky than astral science does to cultivating the land.

2   Many have put horticulture next. But it seems to me good timing *not* to pass on at once to those subjects. I am amazed that some people who look for the charisma of understanding or for the kudos of expertise from these topics have skipped by so many details, making no mention of things that come up by themselves or through garden care. Especially given that the majority of them are accorded more clout than cereals in terms of price and utility for living. And to make a start with acknowledged winners, with items that have filled not only every land but the oceans too, there is a plant that is sown but cannot be cited among cereals or among garden produce: **flax**.[2]

(2) Nature in the garden (19.49–189)

49 It remains to turn back from these plants to *Garden Care*. Its own nature itself makes it a must to recount. Besides which, Antiquity rated no wonder higher than the Garden of the Hesperides, of King Adonis, and of King Alcinous; and the Hanging Gardens – whether built by Semiramis or by Syrus

50 King of Assyria (their work will be the topic of another book of
Pliny).[3] As for the Kings of Rome, they did their own gardening.
Indeed Tarquin the Haughty sent his son back the sadistic and
bloodthirsty message in the story *from the garden*.[4] In our Laws
of the Twelve Tables, nowhere is the word 'farm' used (*uilla*),
but in that sense, 'garden' (*hortus*), and in the sense of garden,
the word 'estate' (*heredium*).[5] This is why a particular sacred aura
has gone along with the garden, and we can see that statues of
satyrs are dedicated only in the garden and in the market-place
as counter-magic against the bewitching powers of those with
the evil eye.[6]

> – Though Plautus does assign Venus as
> tutelary deity of gardens . . .[7]

51 And nowadays under the name 'garden', people own fields and
farms within the city for pleasure. This novelty was first begun
at Athens by Epicurus, Professor of Sloth.[8] Up to Epicurus, it
had not been a custom for people to live in the country within
52 towns. At Rome, the garden was the poor man's field. Ordinary
people got their market produce from the garden.

> – Their diet did so much less harm![9]

It really *must*, I presume, be better to dive down to the depths
and search out the varieties of oyster, shipwreck or no. To go
the other side of the River Phasis for birds that not even the
horrors of myth can protect – in fact all the higher-priced for
it – while other birds are hunted in Numidia and among the
tombs of Ethiopia.[10] To fight wild animals, and get eaten trying
to catch something for someone else to eat.

> – But, by Hercules, what we have here is so cheap, such
> instant pleasure, all anyone could want . . . if the same
> scandal as everywhere else didn't crop up again here.

53 For sure, it would have had to be bearable: growing exotic fruit
that is forbidden to poor people – some for its taste, some for
size, others for being unnatural. Having wine age and lose
potency by going through strainers, while no one's life spans so
long that they never drink wine born before they were. Luxury

dreaming up for itself a porridge from the cereals long ago, and living on just their 'marrow', with the bakeries' creations and etchings for extras – one kind of bread for the high and mighty, another for the folk;[11] and the year's produce going down through so many distinct bands to the common people at the bottom. But has a grid been invented even for plants? Has wealth made discrimination apply even to food which is on sale for a single *as*?

54

The citizen cadres[12] say that some items even among plants don't grow for them – **cabbage** gets fattened to such an extent that a poor man's table can't cope with it. Nature created the '*corruda*' **wild** so that anyone could cut it, but just look: cultivated **asparagus** takes the eye, and Ravenna has a pay-off of three to the pound.

> – Sick, the belly's very own freaks of nature! It would be a stunner for cattle not to be allowed to eat **cardoon thistles** – but the common people *aren't* allowed them![13]

55 Differentials apply to water, too. The very elements of nature are sorted by the power of money. Some drink snow, others ice, turning pain from the hills into pleasure for the gullet. Deep freeze is preserved for the summer heat. The dream is on, of snow cold in months where it doesn't belong. Others boil water – then at once treat it as winter does. Absolutely nothing is liked by mankind just the way Nature likes it.

56

> – Is some plant even going to be nurtured exclusively for the rich man? Won't anyone watch out for the Sacred Mount, the Aventine Hill, and the Plebeian Secessions, wrath of the common people?[14]

The market is *sure* to match people that money has set asunder. Which explains, by Hercules, why no tax at Rome was more important than the market tax in the chants of the common people as they aired their grievances before all the top figures, until the duties on such goods were revoked.[15] The lesson learned was that the rating of wealth cannot be conducted more profitably, more securely, or less at the mercy of Fortune, on any other basis

than this. When that payment is lent to the very poorest people, the guarantor is in the soil, the returns out there in the light
of day, along with the land surface that exults in the sky whatever the weather.[16]

57   Cato gives special mention to garden **cabbages**.[17] In olden days
they used to reckon farmers in terms of their **cabbages**. This
was how they would make an instant judgement that there was
a bad woman in charge inside the home – in fact, this was called
'the female's way to care' – where the garden outside was care-
less. That meant having to live off the butcher's or the market.
They didn't even approve **cabbage** above all else, the way they
do now – they condemned side-dishes that needed another one
on the side, i.e. it was go easy on the olive oil, as a hankering
for fish sauce would even earn a rebuke.

58   The most favoured garden stuff was what needed no fire and
went easy on the wood, an instantly available and ever-ready
asset – which is why **salads** are called 'en vinaigrette',[18] easily
digested, not about to overload the senses with food, the way
to stoke the appetite *least* of all.

Half of 'em relate to seasonings, which amounts to an admission that lending and borrowing at home was the habit, whereas
Indian pepper was no Holy Grail, nor were our other overseas
59   targets. At that time the common people in the city used to
treat their eyes to countryside with an imitation garden every
day in their windows – before a countless horde of rabid
burgling forced all views outside to be blocked up.[19]

On this basis, these items should have their kudos, too. Their
cheapness should not take away their clout – especially when
we observe even the names of top figures grow from them, the
'*Lactucini*' ['the *Les Ttucies*'] in the clan of Valerii weren't
ashamed of their name.[20] And may the effort and caring I have
put in meet with some appreciation.

> – Virgil also owned up how hard it is to
> maintain verbal dignity on such minor topics.[21]

60 § The garden must be **adjacent to the farm-house**. No doubt about it. It should be kept **watered**, if luck is in, best of all by a river that flows past, but if not, then irrigated from a well by using a wheel, wind-machines, or swing-beam scoop.

§ The **soil** must be first **broken up** fourteen days from west wind's coming, as preparation for autumn. The second-time-round dig is before midwinter. A fair rate of work is eight to cover one *iugerum*. **Dung** three feet deep, to mix with earth. Grid in **beds**, ring each of them with tilting 'cushions' making a raised position, and with **paths** along the furrows to grant access for persons and run-off for excess water.

§ A garden grows things that are rated for a variety of reasons – for **bulb, head, stalk** or **leaf** or both, **seed, flesh** or 'gristle' or both, **rind**, or **skin and 'gristle', fleshy casing** . . .[22]

61 § Fruit is variously located: **in the ground, above ground too,** or **only above ground.**

Some grow **lying** horizontal, e.g. **gourd** and **cucumber**, though these also **hang** down, even though they weigh far more than what grows on trees: **cucumber** consists of **gristle and flesh, gourd** of **rind plus gristle**, unique in having **rind** that ripening turns into wood.

62 Hidden **in the ground** are **radishes, navews, turnips**, and, in a different way, **elecampane, rampion, parsnip.**

§ Some I shall label **'fennelesque'**, e.g. **dill, mallow.**

63 NB Experts record that in arabia **mallows** become trees after six months, produce usable walking-sticks. A particular instance of the mallow tree is in Mauretania, at the estuary of the town of Lixus, where the Garden of the Hesperides is claimed to have been:[23] two hundred feet from the ocean, next to a Hercules shrine they say is more ancient than the one at Cadiz. The tree's height twenty feet, in girth beyond anyone wrapping their arms around it.

§ **Hemp**, too, will be put in the same sort of category.

Moreover, we'll also call some things 'fleshy', e.g. 'spongy' plants that grow up in the moisture of meadows.

> NB The leatheriness of **fungi** I spoke of under the *Nature of Wood and Trees*; so, too, in another category, the **truffle**, not long since.[24]

64 § In the class of 'gristle', and **above ground: cucumber.**

> NB The emperor Tiberius took such marvellous pleasure in it, he would seek it out, and in fact on no single day did he not get one.[25] The gardeners moved out into the sun a **cucumber** garden suspended on wheels, and again on wintry days brought them back inside protective see-through sheets.

Why, in the writings of ancient authors of Greece, it says they must be sown with seed soaked for two days in milk/honeyed wine, to make them turn out still tastier.

65 **Cucumber** grows the shape it is forced into. In Italy, green baby ones as tiny as possible are liked; in the provinces, giant waxy or dark ones as huge as possible. Greatest abundance: Africa; greatest bulk: Moesia.[26] When they grow outsize, they are known as '**pumpkins** ripe'. When consumed, they live on in the stomach till the following day, and cannot be passed in among the food, but for all that they aren't very bad for health.

By nature they cannot abide olive oil, to a marvellous degree, but
66 they are equally marvellously partial to water. Snipped off, they still creep towards water that is a fair distance away. Quite the opposite, they shy away from olive oil. If anything gets in the way or if they are hanging, they curve and spiral round. This is detectable within a single night, if a pot of water is put underneath them: they lower four inches before tomorrow comes. But if oil is put there, same method, they curve into 'hooks'. They also grow to a marvellous length if their flower is stuck inside a pipe.

67 > NB Your attention. Stop press: just grown in Campania, a new shape of cucumber – à la quince. I hear it was by chance

that the first one grew like this; right away, its seed created a variety, to be named '**apple pumpkins**'. These don't hang down, they grow into a ball on the ground. Colour: golden. a marvel about them, apart from shape and colour and smell, is that when they reach ripeness, even though not hanging, they leave the pedicle stalk behind.[27]

68 **Columella** hands down his own scheme for **cucumbers** the whole year round:[28] shift the largest possible **bramble** bush to a sunny spot, around the spring equinox, cut back, leaving a stock two inches high. Then in the 'marrow' core of the **bramble**, implant **cucumber** seeds, bank the roots all round with sieved soil and dung, for resistance to cold.

> NB The Greeks have recognized three varieties of **cucumbers**: 'Spartan', 'Skutalik', 'Boeotian'. Of them, only the Spartan sort love water.[29]

> NB Some prescribe soaking their seed before sowing, in the herb named '*culix*', pounded, so as to make them grow seed-less.

69 § **Gourd** is similar in nature, at least in how it grows. Can't abide winter, loves wetting and dung, just as much. Both are sown from seed in a one and a half foot deep ditch in the soil, between spring equinox and summer solstice, but most suitably at the Parilia.[30] Though others prefer sowing **gourds** from 1 March, and **cucumbers** on the 7th and through the Quinquatria festival.[31] They climb up in the same sort of way, tendrils creeping over rough wall surfaces right onto the roof, greed for height being their nature. Their strength needs a prop for standing up, their speed is rapid, covering over vaults and

70 pergolas with a light shade. As a result, there are two basic varieties – '**roof gourd**' and '**common gourd**' (which grows on the ground). The former has a marvellously slender pedicle stalk from which is balanced a weight no breeze can shift.

Gourd also gets to taper in every fashion there is. Mainly through wicker sheaths, interred in them once flowering is over. It grows the shape it is forced into, generally the shape of a coiled snake. If, indeed, it is given freedom to hang, it has been seen nine feet in length.

> NB The **cucumber** flowers one by one. It flowers again on top of its flowers. It tolerates pretty dry spots. Smothered with shining down, all the more while it grows.

71 **Gourds** can be put to a myriad purposes. The first part, the stalk, is food. After that, its nature is utterly different. Recently they have come into use in the baths, instead of pitchers. Since long ago they have served instead of jars, for storing wine. The rind is tender while the plant is green, but nonetheless it is scraped off when it is a question of food. It is healthy and mild in plenty of ways, but still it is among those things that cannot be passed by the human stomach, and swells up instead.

72 The seed which was closest to the neck generates long tall **gourds**. So do those from the bottom, though there is no comparison with the aforementioned. Those mid-way generate round ones. Those at the sides generate thick, shorter ones. They dry in the shade and when you want to sow, they soak in

73 water. For food, the longer and thinner, the more popular, and that is why the ones that have grown hanging are the healthier sort. These also have least seed, the hardness of which restricts its popularity as food.

Those that are kept for seed are by custom not chopped before

74 winter. After that, they dry in smoke, to be country equipment for storing the seeds of garden plants. A system has been discovered to preserve them for food, as well – the same for **cucumber**, too – pretty nearly all the way through to the next cropping. This is done, on the one hand, with brine, and, tradition tells, on the other, they are preserved green in a ditch, at a shady spot, strewn with sand, and covered with dry hay, then earth.

> NB There are also **wild** varieties of both veg., as for virtually all garden plants. But the nature of these too is only medicinal, and for this reason they will be deferred to the books of Pliny where they belong.[32]

75 § All the rest of the plants whose nature is **gristly** are hidden **in the ground**.

§ Among these, I could seem to have said plenty already about **turnips**,[33] if physicians didn't assign masculine gender to the round ones in their number, and feminine gender to the broader and curvaceous ones – that are a class apart in sweetness, and easier to store, but when sown all too often, shift to male gender.

§ The same Greeks have recognized four varieties of **navew**: 'Corinthian', 'Cleonaean', 'Liothasian', 'Boeotian' (which they

76   also call 'the green one').[34] Of these, 'Corinthian' grows to a large size, the root pretty well bare. For this is the only variety that pushes up high, unlike the others, down into the earth. Some call 'Liothasian' *'Thracian'*, the most tolerant of cold that there is. 'Boeotian', though, is sweet, and has a distinctive roundness which is short, not extra long like 'Cleonaean'. Overall, the ones with smooth leaves are also sweeter, the ones with rough, angular, bristle leaves are more bitter.[35]

77   NB There is, besides, a wild variety with leaves similar to **rocket**. At Rome, the 'Amiternum' **turnips** win gold, 'Nursia's' come second, our own ['Roman'] sort are third.[36] The rest of the data on sowing them has been told in the entry on **turnips**.[37]

78   § Consisting of **skin and gristle**: **radishes**. Many of these have thicker skin even than some trees. Their bitterness is extreme, corresponding with the thickness of the skin. The rest of them is from time to time woody. They have a marvellous power of

79   building up wind and releasing belches. For that reason it is ill-bred food, especially if **cabbage** is eaten very soon after – though if radish is eaten with olives just going black, the belching gets spaced out and stinks less.

NB In Egypt **radish** is marvellously acclaimed for the fertility of the oil they make from its seed. They love sowing it most of all, if and when they are allowed, because the profit is greater than from grain, carries lower tax, and no oil there is more plentiful.

80   The Greeks have recognized three varieties of **radish**,[38] each with distinctive leaves – curly, smooth, and, third, the wild sort

81 — the one with smooth leaves, true, but they are shorter, round, abundant, in clumps. Taste actually rough. Like medicine for relaxing bowels. With the two former varieties, however, there is a distinction in terms of the seed, since some bear poor seed, some bear extremely small seed, and both these flaws only afflict the curly leaf variety.

Our own people have recognized other varieties: 'Algidus" (after the place)[39] – a long and see-through sort; a second with a **turnip** shape that they call 'Syrian', pretty well the sweetest, most tender, and superlatively winter tolerant.

> NB Now in fact it looks to have been imported from Syria not so long ago, since it is not to be found in the reference books.[40] Actually lasts the whole winter through.

82 > NB Still there is one further **wild** variety: Greeks call it '*kerais*', the peoples of Pontus '*armos*', others '*leuke*', our language '*armoracia*' – more abundant in leaf than in body.

In trying out all **radishes**, the stalks are inspected above all else, for sour ones have rounder, thicker stalks with long grooves, and the leaves are themselves curlier and 'prickly-angular'.

83 **Radish** wants sowing in loosened, damp soil. It can't abide dung, chaff is enough. So loves cold that in Germany it matches the size of baby boys.[41] Sowing is after the Ides of February, to be for spring, and a second time, around the Feast of Vulcan,[42] the better sowing. Many people also sow in March, April, and September. When development to some size begins, it's a plus to bury every second leaf all round, and earth round the actual radishes, because any that come out above ground will go hard and pitted.

84 Aristomachus prescribes stripping leaves in winter, and preventing pools of standing water by earthing up: that way they grow large in summer.[43] Some have handed down that if a stake is driven in and the hole strewn with chaff to a depth of six inches, then seed is sown into it, and dung and soil piled on, it grows to the size of the pit.

85 However that may be, they are nurtured by salty soil best of all, and so they are also watered with salt water, and in Egypt, where they are best of all for sweetness, sprinkled with soda. Overall, too, their bitterness is removed by saltiness, and they become similar to boiled radishes – when boiled they sweeten and turn into sort-of **navews**.

Physicians advise taking **radishes** raw with salt to draw acid in the guts, and this way they set off movement by repeated vomiting.

86 Tradition says too that this juice is essential for the diaphragm, since the lesson has been learned in Egypt that, once it takes hold inside the heart, nothing else can beat back *'phtheiriasis'* ['the lice disease'], when the pharaohs dissected corpses to investigate illnesses.[44]

Such is Greek empty-headedness, as well, **radish** is said to have been so preferred to all other food that one of gold was dedicated in the temple of Apollo at Delphi, with a **beet** of silver and a **turnip** of lead. You could know for a fact that Manius

87 Curius was *not* born there – the field marshal who, so our histories of Rome have handed it down, was found roasting a **turnip** at the hearth when diplomats from the enemy brought the gold he was going to refuse.[45]

> NB The Greek Moschion also wrote one book *On the Radish*.[46]

> NB They are reckoned the most useful food of all in winter time, and at the same time the eternal enemy of teeth, as they wear them down – for sure they *do* polish ivory.

> NB **Radish** really cannot abide vine – which shies away from any sown nearby.[47]

88 More woody are the rest of the things I put in the '**gristly**' category, and it is a marvel that all of them have a powerful taste.

§ Of these, one variety of **wild, country parsnip** that comes up of its own accord, and a second, from Greece, which roots or sows from seed at the start of spring or in the autumn, as

89 Hyginus advocates,[48] in February, August, September, October, on soil dug over to maximum depth. A yearling starts to be usable, a two year old is more use, more welcome in autumn, above all for casseroles – and still, it has sap that is acrid and hard to cope with.

> NB The **marsh mallow** differs from **parsnip** in being thin – condemned for food, useful for medicine.

> NB There is also a fourth variety, with the same likeness to **parsnip**: known by our folk as 'Gallic', but by the Greeks as '*daukos*', and they have recognized four varieties of it. I must speak of it among pharmaceuticals.[49]

90 § **Rampion** ... has also acquired fame from the emperor Tiberius, who every year insisted on getting it from Germany. A castle set on the Rhine is called Gelduba, and there its breeding is outstanding[50] – which makes it obvious that it suits cold spots. In it, lengthwise, there is a fibre that is pulled out once it is boiled – though a high percentage of the bitterness is left behind, which is soothed with honeyed wine and even turns into something popular, as food.

> NB The larger **parsnip** has the same fibre, at least as a yearling.

Rampion sowing is in February, March, April, August, September, October.

91 § Shorter, more bulging and bitter than these is **elecampane**. On its own it is a stomach's worst enemy; mixed with sweet things it is the healthiest thing going. Once the acidity has been mastered in any from a range of methods, it wins popularity. Gets pounded dry into flour, and soothed with a sweet liquid. Boiled in vinegar, or preserved. Or it soaks in a range of ways, then for mixing with grape syrup, or beaten in with honey, or
92 raisins, or fat dates. Again, another way is blending with quinces or sorbs or plums, and from time to time with pepper or thyme – and this is especially good at giving a failing appetite a fillip, as made famous above all by the daily diet of Julia Augusta.[51]

Its seed is superfluous, since it is sown like a reed by chopping out 'eyes' from the root. Both **elecampane**, **rampion**, and **parsnip** sow at both seasons, spring and autumn, with large gaps between seeds – **elecampane** not less than three feet, as it bushes out far and wide. Better shifting **rampion**.

93 § The next topic is the nature of bulbs. Cato instructs sowing them before all – lauding 'Megarian' ones.[52]

§ But the most prestigious is **squill** – though it is born for medication and sharpening up vinegar. No other has larger dimensions, and likewise with its potent roughness. Two varieties for the pharmacy: male, white leaves; female, dark leaves. Plus a third variety, popular food, known as 'Epimenides'': narrower leaves, less rough.[53]

94 A very great deal of seed in all three – yet those sown from bulbs grown around their sides come up more quickly. To make them grow, leaves – these have large ones – bend down and bury all round. This way, the heads draw all the sap into themselves.

> NB They grow of their own accord in the greatest abundance on the Balearic islands, on Ibiza, and across all Spain.

> NB Pythagoras the philosopher drew up a book on **squill**, systematizing its pharmaceutical powers, and I shall deliver this in my next book.[54]

95 § The rest of the **bulb** varieties differ in colour, size, sweetness – some in fact are eaten raw, as on the Thracian Chersonese,[55] after which the ones that grow in Africa get the best press, closely followed by Apulia's.

> NB The Greeks have recognized the following varieties:[56] 'bolbine', 'setanion', 'opition', 'kuix', 'aegilops', 'sisyrinchion' – in this last, it is marvellous, its lowest roots grow in winter, while in springtime, once violet has appeared, they shrink, while, quite the opposite, the actual bulb fattens up.

96 § Among the varieties is one they call '*arum*' [dragon-root] in Egypt, very close to **squill** in size, to **sorrel** in leaf. Straight

stalk two *cubits* long and the thickness of a walking-stick. Root whose nature is softer, and is even edible raw.

97 § **Bulbs** are **dug** up before spring, or they deteriorate immediately. A sign of ripeness: leaves starting to dry out from the base on up. People grumble at greenish bulbs, ditto long and small ones. Quite the opposite, they admire reddish, rounder, and giant maxi-bulbs. The majority of them have bitterness at the top, while mid-way they are sweet.

> NB Earlier tradition held that bulbs won't grow except from seed, but they grow of their own accord on the plains at Praeneste, and totally out of control in the lands of the Remi.[57]

98 § Pretty well all garden plants have one **root** each, e.g. **radish, beet, parsley, mallow. Sorrel** has the largest – it goes down three *cubits* (smaller in the wild sort). Juicy. Even if dug up, still lives for ages. Yet some have roots **like tresses**, e.g. **parsley, mallow**; some, **twiggy** ones, e.g. **basil**; others, fleshy, e.g. **beet**, or still more so, **saffron**; several consist of **rind and flesh,** e.g. **radish, turnip**; and some others, **jointed**, e.g. **grass**.[58]

99 Plants that have no straight root prop themselves from the outset on a large number of fibres, e.g. **orach** and **blite spinach. Squill**, though, and **bulbs**, and **onion** and **garlic** only root straight down. Some of the plants that grow of their own accord have many many more roots than leaves, e.g. '*spalax*', '*partridge-plant*', **saffron.**

100 § **Flowering.** Bursting into bloom en masse: **wild thyme,** '*habrotonum*', navew, radish, mint, rue. All other plants shed their blossom the moment they start, except **basil**, which does so one by one and starts from the bottom, which is why its flowering lasts the longest. This also happens with the **heliotrope** herb.[59] Some have white flowers, some yellow, some purple.

§ **Shedding leaves.** From the top: **wild marjoram, elecampane**, and **rue** sometimes, when it has suffered rough treatment.

> NB The most concave leaves: **onions**, '*getion*' [*gethyon*] leek.

101 § **Garlic and onions** are counted among divinities in oaths of Egypt. The onion varieties with the Greeks: 'Sardinian', 'Samothracian', 'Alsidenian', this year's '*setanian*', split '*schista*', **'Ascalonian' shallots** named after the town in Judaea.[60]

All have their whole body of rich **gristly** casing, and all, too, have the scent to bring floods of tears, especially 'Cypriots', least of all
102 'Cnidians'. Of them all *setanian* is smallest – except for the 'Tusculan' – but it is sweet. '*Schista*' and 'Ascalonian' get seasoning. '*Schista*' they leave in winter with its tresses, strip the leaves in spring, and others grow up underneath the same incision points – hence, as well, the *name*.[61] With this for blueprint, they bid leaf stripping for the rest of the varieties as well, so they will grow into heads rather than into seed.

103 'Ascalons' have an idiosyncratic nature. For they are, so to speak, infertile from the root, and for that reason the Greeks prescribe they be sown from seed, not putting in the ground, and that, besides, rather late on, around spring. Then when they germinate, get them shifted. This way they start to get fat, and hurry, to compensate for lost time. But with them haste is indeed called for, because they speedily start to rot once ripe. Put in the ground, they send up stalk and seed, but themselves start to disappear.

104 There is also a range of different colours: the whitest ones come up at Issus and Sardis.[62] 'Cretans' also have a reputation – people aren't sure whether these are the same as 'Ascalon' shallots, as the heads get fat if sown from seed, but if set in the ground, stalk and seed get fat.

105 With us, two prime varieties: one for seasoning, which they call '*getion*', but our folk call '*pallacana*', sown in March, April, May; the other forming a head, sown from autumn equinox or west wind's coming, its varieties (in order of acidity): 'African', 'Gallic', 'Tusculan', 'Ascalon's', 'Amiternine'. Best is roundest, likewise red is keener than white, dry than green, raw than cooked/stored.

106 The 'Amiternum' onion sows in cold wet spots, the only one with a head (like **garlic**),[63] whereas all the rest are from seed, putting

out no seed the next summer, but only a head that keeps growing, till the following year there is a switch round and seed grows,
the actual head rots. Therefore, every year seed sown for the onion
is sown separately from seed sown for the seed. They are best pre-
107 served in chaff. *'Getium'* is virtually short of a head, just a long
neck, hence it's all in the leaf, and is regularly chopped back,
like **leek**. Hence they sow this one, too, and don't set it in the
ground.

> NB Otherwisely, they tell us, **onions** sow in thrice dug
> ground, after destroying grass roots, ten pounds per *iugerum*,
> with **savory** mixing in, as it comes up better for it, and as
> well hoeing, four times over, if not more frequently.
> **'Ascalons' shallot** sows in February with our folk, and seed
> harvesting from **onions** starting to go black, before they dry
> out.

108 § In this family, let it be a good moment for discussion of **leek**.
Especially as not long since the emperor Nero gave **chives** clout
by eating them, in olive-oil preserve, on fixed days of each
month, for the sake of his voice – those and nothing else, not
even bread.[64]

Sown from seed after autumn equinox – more thickly if **chives**
109 are wanted. It cuts in the same bed until it fails. Always manured
if being nurtured for heads, before cutting. Once grown, it shifts
to another bed, after the very top of the leaves gently cut back,
above the 'marrow' core, and after the very outside casing peels
back from the head. The ancients used to widen heads by putting
them under a flint or shard – same goes for bulbs – but today
roots gently ease with the hoe, so they arc over, and nourish it,
don't pull it asunder.

110   NB A peculiarity: though it enjoys dung and rich tilth, it
can't abide watered land – . . . and yet they do co-vary with
any particular idiosyncrasies of the soil . . . – the most
admired kind is 'Egypt's'; next, 'Ostia's' and 'Aricia's'.

Two varieties of **chive**: grassy-leaved, with bold grooves on the
leaves, as used by pharmacists; the other one more yellow-leaved,
with rounder, gentler grooves.[65]

NB The tale tells how Mela, from the equestrian order, was summoned by the emperor Tiberius from an appointment as governor. And in utter despair he swallowed **leek** juice weighing up to three silver *denarii*, and died instantly without agony.[66] They do say that a larger measure is not harmful.

111 § **Garlic** is believed to be good, especially, for many a country remedy. It is utterly encased in very fine skins which separate out, followed by numerous interlinked nodes, and these too have separate coatings. Rough flavour, and the more nodes, the rougher it gets. As with **onions**, this too is a nuisance for the breath – but none at all, if cooked.

112   NB Distinguishing feature of the varieties is their timing – early **garlic** ripens in sixty days – and, besides, their size.

§ **Common garlic** is also in this *genus* – the Greeks have dubbed it 'Cypriot garlic', some of them '*antiskorodon*', specially famous in Africa among country platters, larger than garlic. Crushed in oil and vinegar, it builds up a marvellous amount of froth.

Some say *not* to sow **common garlic** and **garlic** on the flat, and tell to put them on little hillocks three feet away from each other, like forts on a wall, four inches between grains; as soon as three leaves burst out, hoeing – they grow larger the more
113 often they are hoed. As they ripen, the stalks press into the ground and bury. This is a precaution against their over-indulgence in leafage. In cold spots, more use sowing in spring than autumn.

NB Otherwisely, so as to lose the stink, all these plants are told to sow when the moon is underground, and to pick when it is in conjunction. Short of all this, one of the Greeks called Menander pledges that **garlic**'s stink dies down if people follow it by eating **beetroot** roasted on hot coals.[67]

114   NB Some people reckon both **garlic** and **common garlic** sow most suitably between the Compitalia and Saturnalia festivals.[68]

Garlic does come up from seed as well, only slowly. The first year its head gets the thickness of leek, the following year it cloves, the third, reaches maturity – and like this it is lovelier, so some people think. Must not go to seed, the stalks must be twisted in a knot for sowing's sake, so the head gets stronger.

115 Now should longer-lasting **garlic** and **onion** be wanted, the heads need soaking in warm salt water. That way they will be longer lasting and better to use – but barren for sowing. Others are happy to hang up first over hot coals, and suppose this ample shift to stop germination – for all that it is certain that **garlic** and **onion** do this even out of the ground, progressively shrinking away as the stalklet enlarges. Some also think **garlic** best preserved in chaff.

116 **Garlic** also occurs **wild** in fields, growing of its own accord – known as '*alum*' – and it is boiled so it can't grow back, and scatter-cast to combat birds eating up seed.

> NB Birds that have swallowed it are at once knocked out and if you hang on a bit they are so drugged they get caught by hand.

There exists another **wild** variety they call 'bear's garlic', same sort of stink, extra thin head, large leaves.

117 § Of plants **sown** in the garden, the **fastest growing: basil, blite spinach, navew, rocket** – bursting out two days on; **dill** – three days; **lettuce** – four; **radish** – nine; **cucumber** – five, **gourd** – six (cucumber gets in first); **cress, mustard** – four; **beet** in summer – five, winter – nine; **orach** – seven; **onions** – 18 or 19; *gethyon* ['*getion*' leek] – nine or eleven. **Coriander** more hard to get, '*cunila*' and **wild marjoram** – a whole thirty days later; least biddable of all **parsley** – nearly forty at its very fastest,
118 and for the most part coming out before fifty. Age of seed is also a factor, as fresh ones grow in better time with: **leek,** *gethyon,* **cucumber, gourd**; while from old seed there come up faster: **parsley, beet, cress,** *cunila,* **wild marjoram, coriander.**

> NB A marvel about **beet** seed, the whole lot does not grow the same year, some comes up the following year, and some

the third – which means that from plenty of seed there only grows a medium amount.[69]

Some seeds reproduce only in the year of their own duration, others do so on several occasions, e.g. **parsley**, **leek**, *gethyon* – sown once, these come up with recrudescent fertility over several years.

119 § **Seeds** of most plants are round, some oblong, a few leaf-like and broad, e.g. **orach**, some narrow and furrowed, e.g. **cummin**. They also differ in colour – black or brighter – and ditto in tough twigginess. They occur in a pouch: **radish**, **mustard**, **turnip**. Bare seed: **coriander**, **dill**, **fennel**, **cummin**. Covered in skin: **blite** spinach, **beet**, **orach**, **basil**. In down: **lettuce**.

120 NB No seed is more fertile than **basil** – instructions say to sow together with curses and insults, to get them growing more happily. After sowing the soil is tamped. **Cummin** sowers also pray it *won't* come up.

NB Seeds inside a rind dry out only with extreme difficulty, most of all **basil**, which is why all these are in fact dried to make them fertile.

In general, plants grow better from seed sown in heaps than from broadcast – at any rate, this makes them sow **leek** and **parsley** fastened in linen rags, **parsley** in a hole made with a dibber, and dung inserted.

121 § All plants grow either from **seed** or from 'avulsion'. Some from both seed and cutting, e.g. **rue**, **wild marjoram**, **basil** – they snip off the top of this too, when it reaches one palm high. Some from both seed and root, e.g. **onion**, **garlic**, **bulbs** and all the yearly producing perennials, with root system intact. Plants that grow from the root have a long-lasting root, and they clump, e.g. **bulbs**, *gethyon*, **squill**. Others clump and have

122 no head, e.g. **parsley**, **beet**. Cutting back the stalk makes pretty well all plants bud again, leaving aside those with a non-rough stalk, and in fact this is put to use, e.g. **basil**, **radish**, **lettuce** – the latter thought even sweeter from secondary growth. **Radish** is in any case nicer when the leaves are pulled

off before it goes to stalk. Ditto for **turnips**, for these too grow after the leaves are pulled off, if earthed over, and then last into summer.

123 § Plants with only **one variety: basil, sorrel, blite** spinach, **cress, rocket, orach, coriander, dill**. These are the same everywhere, no better anywhere than anywhere else.

> NB **Rue** is thought to come up most prolific if it was stolen – just as stolen bees do worst.

> NB Growing whether sown or not: **wild mint, cat mint, endive, pennyroyal**.

By contrast, plants with **lots of varieties**: see above; see below.

124 Pride of place: **parsley**. The sort that grows of its own accord in wet spots is called '*heleoselinum*' ['marsh-parsley', or 'wild celery'], one leaf, non-shaggy.[70] Back in dry spots 'horse-parsley', lots of leaves, but like *heleoselinum*. Third comes '*oreoselinum*' ['mountain-celery'], hemlock leaves, thin root, dill seed, only tinier. The cultivated plant also has a range of varieties, in the leaf – thick, curly, or more sparing and smoother – and ditto the stalk – thinner or thicker, and some have the stalk white, some purple, others variegated.

125 § **Lettuces**. The Greeks recognized three varieties: one, a stalk so broad that it is handed down that garden gate-lets are in production from them – its leaf is slightly bigger than the grass-green variety, and it is very narrow indeed, the growing power presumably having been used up somewhere else. The second, round stalk. The third, known as 'Spartan', squat. Others distinguished varieties by colour and sowing time, there being dark ones whose seed sows in January, blanched ones in March, red in April, all of them with plants for shifting out inside two

126 months. More hard-working people recognize more varieties: purple, curly, 'Cappadocian', 'Greek' – this one with smoother leaf and broad stalk, long, too, and narrow like **endive**. The worst variety they nicknamed '*pikris*' to carry with it a protest against its 'bitterness'. There is a still further category of white, called '*mekonis*' for the 'sleeping-pill' effect of its plentiful 'milk' –

though all are supposed to cause sleep. Among the ancients, this was the only variety of lettuce in Italy, and that's why the word

127 for 'lettuce' comes from 'lac-tic milk'.[71] The purple type with giant root is called 'Caecilian', the round one with dwarf root, broad-leaves, *astutis* ['no-stiffie'], or by some people 'eunuch's lettuce', as it militates most powerfully against lust. All lettuces have a 'cooling-down' nature, hence popularity in summer. They get rid of a belly's jaded appetite, they instil desire for food.

128   NB For sure, the divine Augustus is said to have been saved by lettuce, during an illness, through the wisdom of Dr Musa ['Muse'], when the overdone scruples of his predecessor, Gaius Aemilius, said he must have none.[72] This advert was taken to heart, to such an extent that the invention was made at that time of preserving lettuce into months they don't grow, with honey-vinegar oxymel.

They are also believed to build up your blood.

    NB There is yet a further sort, known as 'goat-lettuce'. I shall discuss it with drugs, below.[73]

    NB Your attention. Stop press: just starting to infiltrate the cultivated lettuce scene, with good reviews, one called 'Cilician': leaf of 'Cappadocian', but curly and broader.

129 § On the one hand it can't be claimed for the same *genus* as lettuce, and on the other it can't be claimed for another: **endive**. – More tolerant of winter, and greater acid content, but stalk just as welcome. Sows from spring equinox, seedlings shift at the end of spring. Also the wild and free endive they call in Egypt '**chicory**', of which more to come elsewhere.[74]

    NB A method has been devised for prolonging all **lettuce** stems and leaves by storing them in jars, boiling them fresh in a pan.

130 § **Lettuce** is sown all year round on rich tilth, well watered and manured, two months each between sowing, seedling, and plant ready. Standard practice, though, to cast seed from midwinter on, to shift seedlings when the west wind comes, or else seed

at the west wind, seedling at spring equinox. Blanched lettuce are most winter-resistant of all.

131　All garden plants love moisture and manure. Especially **lettuce**, and still more, **endive**. Sowing roots smeared in dung is a good idea; so is soil weeding, loosening, and filling up with dung. Some build up their size in other ways, too, cutting them back once grown up to half a foot high, then smearing on pigshit, fresh.

> NB As for bright whiteness, they reckon that it blesses **lettuces** that at least come from white seed, if right from their first growth sand from the shore is heaped round to half their height, and the leaves just shooting up fasten back to the **lettuce** itself.

132　§ **Beet**, smoothest thing in the garden. The Greeks have recognized two varieties of **beet**, too: by colour, black, and white – which they prefer – very sparse for seed – and label 'Sicilian'. (Sure, they *would* use the distinction of shining whiteness in their **lettuce** preferences as well.)

Our people recognize as varieties of **beet** 'spring' and 'autumn', from the sowing seasons, though it sows in June too, and seedlings shift in autumn.

133　**Beet** also love their roots smeared with dung, and a spot just as soaking. Leaves also used to go with lentil and bean, same way as cabbage; the prime method is to pep up their blandness with mustard sharpness. Physicians have judged, **beet** does more harm than **cabbage**, and on that account quite a few people even scruple to taste a serving of it, so they are food specially for the fit and well.

134　Their nature has two sides, combining cabbage and, right at the head as it shoots out, onion bulb. Perfect appearance depends on width, which arrives, as with **lettuce**, by putting a light weight on top once they begin to take on colour. No other garden plant has more width, sometimes a spread of up to two feet, a major factor being the nature of the soil – given that the largest **beet** grow in the territory of Circeii.[75]

135   NB There are those who think **beet** sows best when the pomegranate blossoms, and shifts when they start to have five leaves.

NB One marvellous distinction, if it's true, is that white ones induce passage from the bowels, while black ones restrain it. And when the flavour of wine in a vat spoils with 'cabbage', it is restored by immersing **beet** leaves.

136 § **Cabbage** and **kale**, today emperors of the garden, were not once given respect among the Greeks, my research tells me.[76] Cato, however, pens a marvellous poetic hymn to **cabbage**, which I shall deliver in my chapter on pharmacology.[77] He recognizes as varieties: wide-open leaf and big stalk; a second, curly leaf, they call it *'apiac'* ['parsley-cabbage']; the third, tiny stalk, smooth, tender – his very least favourite.

137 **Cabbage** sows all year round, as it is also cut all year – most usefully, though, from autumn equinox. Shifts when it has five leaves. In the next spring after the first sowing it delivers the sprout-shoot, which is a mini-stalk from the real stalks, super-soft, and extra-tender, disdained by the Sybarite Apicius and (Apicius' doing) Drusus Caesar – with the sequel of a dressing down from his father Tiberius.[78]

138 After the early shoot, from the same **cabbage** summer and autumn sprouts come along, followed by winter sprouts, the second sprout-shoots – no plant *genus* is a match for multi-productivity, only ended when its own fertility uses it right up. Second sowing from spring equinox, the seedling from it plants out at the end of spring, so it won't reproduce from sprout-shoots before it does from stalk. Third sowing around the solstice, seedlings from it plant out, if the spot is on the wet side, in the summer, but if dry, in autumn. If moisture and dung have been short, the flavour is more rewarding, but if they have been plentiful, the yield is happier.

NB Ass dung suits best of all.

139 § This business also numbers among the operations of eatery gluttony, so no one will get fed up if I launch into plenty of verbiage.

Prime **kale** for flavour and size grows if you sow in dug-over soil, then, as they shy from the earth, you keep after the sprouts with earth, and, as they heap themselves up in lush stature, you pile up some more so that no more than the top ever pops out. This variety is called 'Tritian', reckon the cost and irk at 100 per cent extra.

140 The rest of the varieties are numerous: 'Cumaean', squat leaves, spreading head; 'Arician', no taller in height, more leaves, but not more tender leaves – thought most useful of all because under almost all leaves it clumps extraordinary sprouts. 'Pompeian' is taller, with a thin stalk from the root up and thick growth between leaves – rather few and far between and on the narrow side, yet their tenderness is a treasure; non-cold-resistant. Whereas 'Bruttians' are actually nurtured by cold, outsize leaves, thin stalk, sharp flavour. 'Sabellian' has utterly marvellous leaves, they're so curly, and their thickness whittles down the actual

141 stalk – but talk says they are sweetest of the whole lot. Recently, 'Lacuturnians' from the valley at Aricia have shown up, outsize head, countless leaves, some gathered in a ball, others bulging sideways; no others have more head, after the 'Tritian', which can be seen at times a foot across and is later than none with the sprout-shoot stage.

142 Whatever the variety, hoar frosts are the largest factor in making them sweet, but once they are cut they do enormous harm – unless the 'marrow' core is protected by making the scar go crosswise. Ones marked out for seed are *not* cut.

> NB One variety has its very own popularity – it never outgrows the look of a seedling. They call it *'halmuris'* ['salty', sea-kale] as it will not come up except in coastal areas. They say that these keep safe and green through no matter how long a voyage, if the instant they are cut they never once touch the ground, but are stored in oil-jars dried out as freshly as possible, then stoppered with all the air locked out.

143 There are people who think the seedling gets faster to ripeness if, in shifting it, seaweed is put under the pedicle stalk, or as

much soda powder as three fingers can hold; and others who spray leaves with powdered trefoil seed and soda.[79] In cooking, soda safeguards greenness, too – as in Apicius' recipe of soaking in oil and salt before cooking.[80]

144   NB There is a style of 'grafting' veg. to veg., by snipping short shoots and adding seed from other plants into the 'marrow' of the stalk. The same as with **wild cucumber**.

NB Here is one more **wild cabbage** to add: given exceptional publicity in the soldiers' comic chants at the triumph of the divine Julius Caesar, which had them rebuke him in call and answer verses for making them live on *'lapsana'* at Dyrrachium, in protest at his low-budget rewards.[81] This variety is a wild sprout.

145 § The most lavish care of all the things in the garden goes on **asparagus**.

NB Its origination from **wild** *'corruda'* has had the full treatment, plus the way Cato tells to sow it in reed-beds.[82]

NB There is another variety, less cultivated than asparagus, milder than *corruda*, that grows all over, even up in the hills – the plains of Upper Germany are crammed, and, according to a far from glib witticism of Tiberius Caesar, there is a plant grows there that is just like **asparagus** – it's a weed.[83]

146   NB Actually, the one that grows of its own accord on Nesis, the island in Campania, is rated best of all.

The garden variety sows from 'sponges', as it has lots and lots of root, germinates deepest of all. Goes green when the stem first pops up, shooting the stalk up, and in the same phase tapering into fluted bulges.

147 It can also sow from seed. Cato gives nothing more hard-working coverage, and it's the last thing in his book, so it's obvious it was just creeping in then, and the new thing.[84] He tells to get a spot dug over that is moist or thick, sowing at half a foot intervals on all sides, so it doesn't get trodden on, and besides,

along a line, two or three grains will press down with a dibber
– evidently, at the time they were only sown. This to get done
148 after spring equinox, manure saturation, intensive tidying,
taking care the **asparagus** does not pull up with the weeds.
First year: protection from winter with straw, uncovering in
spring, hoeing, weeding; year three, spring: burning off. The
more speedily it is burned off, the better it comes up, so it suits
reed beds most of all, as they get a move on when they burn.

The same expert tells, no hoeing before the **asparagus** grows, so
149 the roots don't get disturbed in hoeing; next, pulling **asparagus**
from the root, for if they are snapped off, they run to stalk and
die down. Pulling till it goes to seed – it gets to ripen towards
spring – and burning off, then again when the **asparagus** has
shown, hoeing and manuring. Nine years on when it has aged,
splitting off on dug-over and manured soil, then sowing from
'sponges' with a one-foot gap each.

NB Specifically: use sheep heaps, as anything else breeds
weeds.

150 Nothing tried since that time has been found more useful, except
that they sow around the Ides of February, digging the seed in
heaps in tiny ditches, maximum soaking in dung. Then 'sponges'
form, after autumn equinox, from the intertwining of roots, and
they put out at one-foot intervals, fertility lasting ten years each.

151 NB I already noted, no soil more welcome to **asparagus**
than in the gardens of Ravenna.[85]

NB '*Corruda*' – by this I understand wild asparagus that
the Greeks call '*horminos*', '*muakanthos*', and other names –
I am informed, also grows if rams' horns crush and dig in.

152 § Everything that has value might now seem to have been
discussed – if there weren't something left where profits are huge
but it can't be discussed without shame.

Cardoon artichokes. It is a sure fact, at great Carthage, and
Corduba especially, **cardoons** bring six thousand *sesterces* from
small beds – as we turn the whole earth's freaks of nature into

eatery gluttony, and even sow stuff that makes all quadrupeds shy away.

153 **Cardoons**, then. Two ways, autumn as seedling, and as seed before the Nones of March[86] – seedlings from that set out before the Ides of November, or in cold spots, around west wind's coming. They manure too, and, gods willing, come up the happier. They also store in honey-vinegar dilution with laser-wort root and cummin added – so no day has to get by without an artichoke thistle.

154 § **The rest** can be treated to a flying visit:

§ **Basil** sows best, they say, at the Parilia Festival,[87] some adding, plus autumn, and tell, when sowing for winter, to douse seed in vinegar.

§ **Rocket** and **cress** as well grow perfectly readily in summer or winter. **Rocket** is special – 'cold-shoulderess' of winter and, its nature quite the opposite of lettuce, 'starter-motoress' of lust.
155 This is why it usually pairs up with lettuce for food, so excess chill can mix in equivalent heat, and the blend balance out moderation. **Cress** got its name, '*nasturtium*', from 'nostril torture' ['*nares* + *torqueo*'], and so it is the meaning 'energy' has appropriated the word for the common phrase, as if to say 'wake up, lazybones'.[88]

NB In Arabia it is said to grow to a marvellous size.

156 § **Rue**, too, sows from west wind's coming, and from autumn equinox. Cannot abide winter, damp, dung. Loves sunny, dry spots, earth with maximum brick content. Wants nurturing with ash – and this also mixes with seed, to be caterpillar-free.

NB It had special clout with the ancients. I am informed that honeyed wine with rue flavour was handed out to the people by Cornelius Cethegus, colleague of Quintus Flaminius in the consulate, on completing the elections.[89]

NB Its alliance with the fig is so strong that it comes up happier nowhere than under this tree.

157 **Rue** also sows from a cutting. Better if inserted into a hole in a bean, which nurtures it with juice, tightening its grip on the cutting. It sows itself, too: as the end of any branch arcs over, once it touches the ground it instantly roots.

> NB **Basil** has the same nature – except the seed dries less readily.

Rue weeding is not without awkwardness: ulcers itch if it isn't done with protection for the hands, or a barrier of olive oil for them.

> NB Its leaves also store, they keep in bundles.

158 § **Celery**[90] sows from spring equinox, from seed ground a little in a mortar. This way they think they grow more curly – or if once sown it is trodden in, using roller or feet.

> NB It has the kudos in Achaea of crowning winners in the holy games at Nemea.[91]

159 § Same sowing time for **mint**, from seedling or, if not yet budding, from 'sponge'. Less than keen on damp ground. Green in summer, turning yellow in winter.

Wild mint variety: '*mentastrum*'. Propagation from this à la vine, or turn sprays upside down and sow.

> NB Among the Greeks the sweetness of its scent has changed its name, as at other times it was called '*mintha*', the source of our ancestors' modification of the name, whereas now it is coming to be known as '*heduosmos*' ['sweet-smeller'].

160 NB Popular for stuffing furnishings, and the scent goes all round the table at a country feast.

Sown the once, it lasts a long long time.

> NB It is linked to **pennyroyal**, whose nature – it flowers inside a larder! – has been discussed several times.[92]

> NB Also these are preserved in the same style – I mean **mint**, **pennyroyal**, and **cat mint**.

§ Though of all[•••]seasonings that[•••]jaded palates[•••],
161 **cummin** is the best ally.[93] It grows only just clinging to ground
surface, and straining up high, in crumbly soil, and the warmest
possible spots, for mid-spring sowing.

> NB The other variety of it is the **wild cummin** they call
> 'country' cummin, others say 'Theban'.[94] When its powder
> is drunk in water for stomach-ache, cummin from
> Carpetania gets the highest ratings in our Romanized world,
> elsewhere the prize goes to 'Ethiopian' and 'African' – some
> preferring 'Egyptian' to the latter.

162 § Now black **alexanders** has an extraordinarily marvellous
nature – Greeks call it '*hipposelinum*' ['horse parsley'], others
'*smurnaion*' ['myrrhesque']. Grows from tears wept from its
stalk,[95] sows from root too.

> NB Those who gather its sap say it has a myrrh flavour, and
> Theophrastus pledges, it grew from sown, garden, myrrh.[96]

163 The ancients instructed sowing **horse parsley** on uncultivated
stony spots beside a stone wall. Today it also sows on a trenched
spot, from west wind's coming after autumn equinox. That was
because **caper** also sows mainly at dry spots, on a bed hollowed
down for digging, with banks built all round from stones.
Otherwise it goes on the loose through all the fields, and forces
the soil to go barren. Flowers in summer, grows green right
through to the Pleiads' setting,[97] most at home on sandy spots.

> NB The bad points of the one that grows overseas I discussed
> in with *Exotic Shrubs*.[98]

164 § Also exotic is **caraway**, called after the name of its country.
first and foremost for the kitchen. Will grow in any land at all,
on the same basis as **alexanders** – highest ratings, though, for
caraway in Caria, second in Phrygia.[99]

165 § **Lovage** ['*ligusticum*'] is wild in the hills of Liguria, its home.
Sows all over, the cultivated the sweeter, but lacks gusto.

> NB Some call it '*panax*' ['all-heal']. Crateuas,[100] among the
> Greeks, calls 'cow *cunila*' by that name, where others say

'*conyza*', i.e. '*cunilago*', and what is '*cunila*', '*thymbra*'. Among us, '*cunila*' savory has another name too, called '*satyreia*', under the category of seasonings.

§ '*Cunila*' sows in February, rival of **wild marjoram**. Nowhere gets both of them added together – their contribution is indeed similar, though only Egyptian **wild marjoram** is ranked above *cunila*.

166 § Another exotic was, formerly, **pepperwort**. Sows from west wind's coming. Then when it has clumped, chops off close to the ground. Then weeding, manuring. They use it, same clumps, for two years thereafter, if a cruel winter doesn't blitz it, since it has minimal cold resistance. It grows up to a *cubit* height, bay leafed only softer. Its use is non-milk-free.

167 § **Git** grows for the baker's, **anise** and **dill** for kitchen and pharmacy, '*sacopenium*' leavens **laserwort**, it *is* in the garden but only as a drug.

§ There are some plants that **accompany the sowing of others**, e.g. **poppy** – sown with **cabbage** and with **purslain**; and **rocket**
168 with **lettuce**. Three varieties of cultivated **poppy**: white, the seed of which was among the ancients served roasted for the second course with honey, and it is sprinkled over the crust of a country loaf, sticking on, in an egg paste, while **parsley** and **git** season the bottom crust with Ceres' very own flavour.[101] The second variety of **poppy** is black, its stem slits and out comes milky juice. The third variety the Greeks call '*rhoeas*', our people call it
169 '*wandering*' **wild poppy** – does grow on its own accord, but for the most part in with barley in the fields. Looks like **rocket**, a *cubit* in height, flower red and drops off at once, which is where it got its name from the Greeks.[102]

> NB The rest of the varieties of **poppy** that grows of its own accord I shall discuss in the section *On Pharmacology*.[103]

> NB It has always had kudos among the Romans: the proof is Tarquinius Superbus, who by shaking off the tallest **poppies** in the garden handed the diplomats sent by his son the famous bloody reply in silent riddle form.[104]

170 § Again in another posse, sowing at autumn equinox: **coriander, dill, orach, mallow, sorrel, chervil** – Greeks call it *'paideros'*[105] – and, with keenest flavour, fiery impact, and best for bodily health, **mustard**, needing no cultivation, though better shifted as seedling, but, look, on the other side, it is hardly possible once it is sown to get the spot free of it, as the

171 seed grows green as it drops. Its use is as a side-dish, boiled down in pans till the pungency is the other side of detectable. Leaves boil as well, like the rest of the veg. They have three varieties: one thin, the second like turnip leaves, the third like rocket's. Best seed from Egypt.

> NB Athenians named it *'napu'*, others *'thlaspi'*, others *'saurion'*.

172 § **Thyme** and **wild mint** teem on most hills, e.g. in Thrace, so people fetch down sprays pulled off them, to sow, and ditto at Sicyon from *its* hills, and at Athens from Hymettus. In the same sort of way they sow wild mint too, but it is happiest to grow on the walls of wells, around fishponds and pools.

173 § **The remainder** belong to the *genus* 'fennel', as e.g. **fennel** itself, most popular with snakes, as I have said, useful for seasoning most things once dried.[106] And very like it, *'thapsia'*, which I discussed in *On Exotic Shrubs*,[107] and **hemp**, the most useful plant for ropes.

Hemp is sown from west wind's coming, the more thickly, the more tender. Seed, once ripe, is stripped from autumn equinox on, then sun, wind, or smoke dried. **Hemp** itself is pulled up after the grapes are in, and cleaned in late-night sessions of peeling.

174 The best are from Alabanda, specially for use in nets. Three varieties of it there: what is closest to the cortex skin or to the 'marrow' core is deplored, highest rated is from half way, called *'mesa'*. Second is 'Mylasa's'. So far as growing tall is concerned, 'Rosea's', on Sabine land, matches a tree's height.[108]

175 § The two varieties of **giant fennel** I have discussed under *Exotic Shrubs*.[109] In Italy its seed is food, it is stored in jars, and lasts

even a year's duration. Two product types from it, stalks and clusters. They call it '*korumbia*', and [the 'clusters'] they store '*korumboi*'.

176 § **Diseases** afflict garden plants, just the same as other plants sown in the ground. Thus **basil** regresses in old age into **wild thyme, wild mint** into '*zminth*', and **turnips** come from old **cabbage** seed, and so forth. **Cummin** is killed by '*haemodoron*', unless cleaned off – single stemmed, root like a bulb, growing exclusively in thin soil. Another individual disease of **cummin** is scabbing. **Basil** goes pale at the Dog Star's rising.[110]

NB All go yellow at a menstruating woman's approach.

177 Varieties of **minibeast** also grow on them, 'flea' crawlies on **navews**, 'rocket' creepies and maggots on **radish**, ditto **lettuce** and **cabbage**, both of them worse than **radish** for slugs and snails, **leek** too has its own special creatures – caught very easily indeed, by dressing dung on top as they bury themselves in it.[111]

NB It doesn't help, either, iron touching **rue**, *cunila*, **mint, basil**, so Sabinus Tiro pledges in his book '*Kepourika*' (*On Gardening*) that he dedicated to Maecenas.[112]

178 NB The same expert published a remedy against **ants**, high toll agent of mass destruction in the garden, if not well watered: sea mud or ash, for blocking their holes. But the most effective way to kill them is with the **heliotrope** plant. Some think a water with raw brick clay wash is their enemy.

179 Therapeutic for **navew**: some **bitter vetch** in with it, as **chick-pea** with **cabbage**, which keeps **caterpillars** away, but if they do crop up because this wasn't done, treatment is to spray on boiled **wormwood** sap or *sedum*'s – the *genus* of herb, as I said,
180 some call '*aeizoon*'.[113] If **cabbage** seed is sown soaked in its juice, tradition says, the cabbages will be vulnerable to no creatures.

NB And in general, **caterpillars** are killed if there is fixed on a pole in the garden a horse skull, or at any rate a mare's. Against **caterpillars**, too, the tale is told, a river crab hung up at the garden's centre is a help.

NB There are those who touch what they want to be invulnerable to **caterpillars** with blood-red twigs.

Gnats as well infest a well-watered garden, especially if there is a shrubbery. Burning **galbanum** resin shoos them.

181 Now as far as the **decomposition of seeds** is concerned, some of them have greater stability, e.g. **coriander, beet, leek, cress, mustard, rocket,** *cunila*, and in general the acidic ones. Less stable: **orach, basil, gourd, cucumber,** and all summer seeds more stable than winter's. Least durable: *gethyon*. None of even the strongest of them is usable beyond four years, for sowing at any rate. For the kitchen they are still in season even beyond that.[114]

182 Specially therapeutic for **radish, beet, rue,** and *cunila* is salt **water**, which in other areas as well contributes hugely to sweetness and fertility. Watering with fresh water does the rest of the plants good, the most useful being the coolest and sweetest to drink; less useful, water from a pond or brought in by runnels, as they fetch in weed seeds – though rainwater does nurture best, as it kills the minibeasts growing on them.

183 **Times of day to water** the garden: morning and evening, so the water won't evaporate in the sun. For just **basil**, add mid day too – as they think, it bursts out with all speed even once sown, if sprayed with boiling water at the start.

All the **plants** grow better and bigger if **shifted**, most of all **leek** and **navew**. There is a curative power in shifting, they stop feeling wounds, e.g. *gethyon*, **leek, radish, parsley, lettuce, beet, cucumber**.

184 Pretty well all **wild plants** are smaller in leaf and stalk, more acid in juice, e.g. *cunila*, **wild marjoram, rue**. The only one of them all where the wild one is better is **sorrel**, known as '*rumix*' in its cultivated sort, strongest of all the plants that are sown and grow. Tradition, for sure, tells that sown once it

185 persists, is never defeated, everlasting most of all beside water. Its use: only as food, together with **pearl barley** – makes the flavour gentler and more pleasant. The wild sort is useful for many medications.

NB To such an extent has caring left nothing undone that I find it expressed in a poem,[115] if individual 'beans' of goat dung are hollowed, and seeds of **leek, rocket, lettuce, parsley, endive, cress** are locked in and sown, they come up marvellously.

For plants where there are wild ones, they are perceived to be drier and more acid than cultivated ones.[116]

186 Now the range of different **juices and flavours** needs discussion, wider with these plants than with orchard fruits.[117] Acid ones: *cunila*, **wild marjoram, cress, mustard**; bitter: **wormwood, centaury**; watery: **cucumber, gourd, lettuce**; sharp: **thyme**, *'cunilago'*; sharp and scented: **parsley, dill, fennel**. Of the flavours, the only one that does not grow is ready-salted. Sometimes it settles on top outside, like dust – and only for wee **chick-pea**.

187 And to make sure living opinion is seen to be hollow, more often than not, **all-heal** gives a pepper flavour, and still more does *'siliquastrum'* [**pepperwort**], getting the name *'piperitis'* on that account. *'Libanotis'* [**rosemary**] gives a **frankincense** scent, *'zmyrnium'*, **alexanders**, that of **myrrh**. *'Libanotis'* sows in crumbly, meagre, dewy spots. On **all-heal**, plenty has been said before.[118] It has an **alexanders** scent, no different than **frank-**
188 **incense**. Its use after a year is very healthy for a stomach. Some call it another name, **rosemary** ['sea dew']. The herb **alexanders** sows in the same spots, and tastes of **myrrh** in the root. Same sowing for **pepperwort**. The rest differ from all others, in scent and flavour both, e.g. **anise**. And the diversity and strength are so strong that not only is one modified by another, but gets utterly effaced. Cooks remove vinegar from dishes with **parsley**, and storekeepers remove a heavy smell from wine, with the same plant, in bags.

189 § At this point ends discussion of **Garden Plants**, at least for the sake of food. The most important work of nature remains for the same things, since I have dealt with only their *produce*, and some of the *gist*, whereas the true nature of each one can only be fathomed through their *therapeutic* impact, a vast work than which none more huge could be hit on.

A well-judged strategy has meant I'm *not* interweaving this topic with the individual things, because desire for healing is relevant to a different set of people, and both would have suffered long delays if we had mixed them up. As it is, each thing will settle in its own sector, and people who want can match them up.

Plate 7 The Rustic Calendar mosaic at Saint-Romain-en-Gal. *C*. 200–225 CE. 0.52m². Musée des Antiquités nationales, Saint-Germain-en-Laye, Paris.

4

WITH PALLADIUS

A year in the garden

THE WORK OF AGRICULTURE (SELECTIONS ON THE GARDEN)

(1) On the spot for a garden and an orchard, on hedges and sowing (1.34)

1 § **Garden** and **orchard** must be very close to home – the garden best of all lying below the byre, whose liquid feed will of its own accord fertilize it. **Sited** a long way from the threshing floor, as it finds chaff dust hostile.

2 § A good luck site has a gently sloping level which sluices off channels of running **water** through zoned areas. If a spring is lacking, either a well needs sinking or, if you can't manage this, a fishpond must be built higher up, so that when rainfall brings it in water, the garden is watered through the heat of summer. If you lacked all these possibilities, you'll dig a little garden three or four foot down,[1] just like trenching – cultivated this way it can forget about spells of drought.

3 NB Although any type of earth suits this if helped by dung to counter need, yet these kinds are to be avoided if there's a choice: the clay we call potter's, and 'red earth'.

For a garden unaided by natural water, you'll keep watch on turning the space for cultivation with half in winter to south, half in summer to north.

4   § There are many varieties of **enclosure**. Some people mock up partly shaped walls with clay squared off in frames; those who have the means raise stone walls from clay and stone; the majority build up rocks piled in a row without clay.

> NB Quite a few people edge the space for cultivation with ditching, but this is to be avoided because it removes moisture from the garden, unless the cultivated spot happens to be marshy.

5   § Others set out **thorn** seedlings and seed as walling. But it will be better to collect ripe **bramble** seed, and the seed of the thorn called **dog thorn**, and mix in with **vetch** flour soaked in water; then introduce old ropes of broom with this style of mixture, so that seed is taken up within the ropes, and kept safe right through to the start of springtime.

6   Next, in the place where the **hedge** will be, we'll make two furrows, three feet apart and one and a half in depth, and along both of them we'll bury the ropes with a light soil covering.

This way in thirty days the **briars** come up – while tender they need the help of props – and they'll interlink with each other across the spaces left empty.

7   § **Divisions** of the garden, for sure, need making in such a way that those in which sowing will be in autumn are trenched in springtime; those we'll fill with seed in spring, we must dig up in autumn. This way both trenched plots will break down organically thanks to cold or sun.

Beds need making, narrow and long, i.e. twelve foot long and six wide, divided this way for cleaning the area from both sides. Their edges shall be raised two feet in damp or irrigated spots; in dry ones it will be enough to lift them one foot.

Spaces between beds, if water habitually flows away, will have to be higher than the actual beds, so that water admitted to the bed from greater altitude will get in more readily, and when it has satisfied the bed's thirst, can be shut out and diverted to others.

8 § Though I assign fixed **sowing times** by the month, still every single individual shall keep watch on them in accordance with the nature of the spot and the weather.

In cold spots, autumn sowing shall be sooner, and the spring one later; in hot regions, the autumn sowing can be later too and the spring one earlier. Whatever is for sowing shall be sown at the waxing of the moon; what is for cutting or gathering, at the waning.

(2) On garden and farming remedies (1.35)

1 § To counter **cloud**, and **rust**, you shall burn up chaff and refuse set out at lots of spots throughout the garden, all of it at once, when you see the cloud on its way.

§ To counter **hail**, many ideas are mentioned: a millstone is covered with a crimson rag. Likewise bloodied axes are raised menacingly against the sky. Likewise all the space of the garden is edged with **white bryony**, or a bat is nailed up outstretched and spread-eagled, or the tools to work with are oiled with bear

2 tallow. Some keep bear lard beaten in olive oil, and they oil sickles with this when about to do pruning.

> NB But this remedy has to be kept secret so no pruner can realize. Its power is held to be so great that it cannot be harmed by freeze, by cloud, by any creature. It matters that the thing has no strength *if divulged*.

§ To counter **gnats** and **slugs** we either spray fresh olive dregs or soot from the ceiling.

§ To counter **ants**, if they have a hole in the garden, we shall attach a bat's heart; if they come from outside, we'll mark the whole garden space with ash or white chalk.

3 § To counter 'rocket' crawlies, seeds for scattering shall be soaked with the sap of **live-for-ever** [houseleek], or the blood of 'rocket' crawlies. **Chick-pea** is for sowing among veg. on account of many prodigies. Some scatter ash from fig wood on the *'rocket'* crawlies. Likewise they sow **squill** in the garden or at least hang it up.

NB Some make a woman who is having her period walk round the garden, no ties round her anywhere, hair loose and feet bared, to counter 'rocket' crawlies, et cetera.

4 § To counter creatures that **harm vines**, you'll plunge the blister-beetles that we're used to finding on **roses**, in olive oil, let them dissolve away, and then when the vines are for pruning you'll anoint sickles with this oil.

Bed-bugs are killed off in beds, and spots oiled with olive dregs and cattle bile, or with mashed **ivy** leaves on olive oil, or burned leeches.

5 § So veg. won't breed hostile creatures, sow in a tortoise-shell all the seed you're going to scatter dry, or else **mint** in lots of places, but most of all among the **cabbage**. It's said, this results from a little scattering of **vetch**, specially where **radish** and **turnip** grow.

A mixture of sour vinegar, it's said, with **henbane** sap kills 'flea' crawlies, if you sprayed.

6 § Someone conquers **caterpillars**, it's said, by burning up headed stocks of **garlic** through the whole garden space, and getting stench up at a number of spots. If we're looking after vines, it's said, pruning hooks need oiling with ground **garlic**. They're also stopped from growing if you burned tar and sulphur around the shanks of fruit-trees or vines, or if you remove **caterpillars** from a garden next door, boil them in water, and pour it all over your entire garden space.

§ So **blister-beetles** don't harm vines, they need squashing on the whetstone that sharpens the sickles.

7 § Democritus insists[2] that no harm can be done to fruit-trees or plants by any creatures whatsoever, *if* you put in water, in an earthen pot, loads of river or sea crabs, called by the Greeks *'pagouroi'*, not less than ten of them, and stick them out in the open, so that in ten days they steam in the sun; then afterwards you drench whatever you want to be unharmed, repeating this after eight days are up each time, until the things you want grow up firm.

8 § **Ants** you'll drive away by spraying the hole with ground **wild marjoram** and ground sulphur. This also harms bees. Likewise if you've burned empty snail shells and heel the ash into the hole.

§ **Gnats** are shooed by pouring on *galbanum* resin or sulphur; 'flea' crawlies, with olive dregs regularly sprayed over paved flooring, or with **wild cummin** ground up with water, or frequent pouring on of **wild cucumber** seed softened in water, or else lupine broth boosted with the dryness of *'psilothrum'* [**white bryony**].

9 § **Mice**, if you pour thick olive dregs on a dish and place this in the house at night, they'll stick to it. Likewise they'll be killed, if you mix cheese or bread or lard or barley-meal with dark **hellebore**, and put it out for them. A potion of **wild cucumber** and *'colocynth'* will hurt them this way.

> NB Against field mice, Apuleius insists[3] that seeds are for soaking in cattle bile before you broadcast them.

Quite a lot of people block their holes with **oleander** leaves – they die through these while they struggle to get out.

10 § **Moles** the Greeks pursue in this style: they tell, to bore a hole in a nut or any variety of fruit with the same hardness; chaff and cedar resin with sulphur to be enclosed inside, the right amount; then all the moles' tiny entrances and the rest of their breathing vents to be buried over carefully; one hole, a big one, to be kept safe, and at its entrance a nut with fire burning inside to be positioned so that it can take in puffs on one side, and pour them out of the other; when the burrows are filled with smoke this way, moles either run off right away or are killed.

11 § **Field mice**, if you stuff their entrances with oak ash, through regular contact scabbing will take hold and destroy them.

§ **Snakes** are shooed by virtually any acridity – harmless heavy-smelling smoke drives off harmful spirits. Let's burn *galbanum* resin or stag horns, lily roots, nanny-goat hooves. In this fashion harmful monsters are repelled.

12   § The view of the Greeks is that, if a 'cloud' of **locusts** suddenly arises, it can pass by – *if* all the humans lurk under their roofs. But if they catch people who don't spot them out in the air, no fruit is harmed – *if* they all run away indoors at once. They are said to be driven off by bitter **lupine** or **wild cucumber** elixir, if it's set up mixed with brine.

Some reckon that **locusts** or **scorpions** can be shooed if some of them burn in their midst.

13   § **Caterpillars** quite a few people pursue with fig ash. If they persist, some shall boil up in cattle urine and olive dregs mixed in equal proportions; then, when they cool, spray all veg. with this liquid.

> NB The Greeks call some creatures which habitually harm the garden *'prasokourides'* ['leek shearers'].

So you'll have to cover lightly the paunch of a wether, at the instant of slaughter, still full of its waste, in the space where they are teeming. After two days you'll find the actual creatures in heaps. When you've done this two or three times, you eliminate the whole species that was doing harm.

14   § It is believed that it blocks off **hail** if someone carries round a crocodile- or hyena- or sea cow-skin through the extent of the estate, and hangs it up at the entrance to farmhouse or farmyard, when they see a blight loom. Likewise if they carry by hand a marsh tortoise on its back, walk through the vineyard, returning in the same way, and set it on the ground – in such a way as to put clods against the curvature of its back so it can't overturn, but is permanently face up. Doing this, it's said, makes the hostile cloud hurry past a space defended this way.

15   Some people, when they see the blight loom, present a mirror and take in the cloud's image. This remedy averts the cloud – doesn't it like it when it runs into itself, or does it yield as if to its double?

Likewise a sea cow-skin thrown over one vine plant, at a spot in the centre of the vineyard, is believed to cloak the limbs of the whole vineyard against looming blight.

16   § All garden or farm seed is said to be kept safe from all blights and monsters, if they're soaked first in ground **wild cucumber** root.

Likewise the skull of a mare, one that has foaled, is for putting in the garden – or, better, an ass's. Through their presence, they are believed to fertilize the things they look upon.

(3) Month of January (2.14)

1   § **Lettuce** is for sowing in January or December, so its seedling will shift in February. Likewise sows in February, so it can shift in April. But it's a fact that it sows well all year round, if the spot is in good heart, manured, watered.

Before fixing in place, we shall chop back its roots level and smear with liquid dung, or ones that are already fixed in shall uncover and take manure. Loves well-dug soil, rich, moist, manured.

2   Weed between **lettuces** is for pulling up by hand, not by hoe.

Gets broader if put in thin, or if, when it starts to produce stalk, the stalk is lightly nicked, and the lettuce squashed with a clod or sherd. They are thought to grow blanched if river or shore sand is frequently scattered on their hearts, and the leaves are bunched to fasten them up.

3   If through fault of soil, season, or seed, **lettuce** hardens quickly, its seedling will pull out, put in afresh, and attain tenderness.

Likewise it will grow tender when put in with many seeds, if you hollow out a goat shit pellet fine with a cobbler's awl, and insert in it seed of **lettuce**, **cress**, **basil**, **rocket**, **radish**, then wrap up the pellet in dung, and plunge it down in best-cultivated earth, in a low pit. **Radish** works into the root, the other seeds pop up at the surface as the **lettuce** emerges in step with them, keeping

4   the individual flavours. Others achieve this as follows: they pull up a **lettuce** and pluck the leaves that are joined to roots: in the same positions, pricking these with a stick, they put in the aforementioned seeds, apart from **radish**, and smear on dung. **Lettuce** re-buried this way will be surrounded by stalks from the aforementioned seeds.

NB 'Lettuce' ['*lactuca*'] is so named because it overflows with an abundance of milk ['*lac*'].

5   § This month, and at any time, **cress** must by common consent be set in, at any spot you please, and whatever the weather. Doesn't want dung. Though it delights in moisture, still it doesn't care if there's a dearth of it. If it sows with **lettuce**, it's said to grow exceptionally well.

§ Both now and any month or spot you like, don't hesitate to sow **rocket**.

§ This month too and all year round **cabbage** can sow — but better in the other months it has been prescribed for.

§ This month too **garlic** and **wild garlic** will sow well — but white earth will benefit **garlic**.

(4) Month of February (3.24)

1   § Around the Ides of February garden **hedges** must be made from **thorn** seed heaped on ropes, as stated when I was speaking of garden defences.

Likewise the Greeks say that a whopping **bramble** twig must be made into little bits, buried in pits a palm deep, and nurtured daily until it has leaves, with digging and watering.

2   § This month **lettuce** sows, so it can shift in April. Likewise **artichoke** sows, and **cress**, **coriander**, **poppy**, as in November, and **garlic** or **wild garlic**.

§ Now **savory** sows on rich land, not manured, but sunny, or better very close to the sea. It shall sow mixed with a few **onions**.

3   § This month too you sow **onions**, but all agree it is for sowing in both spring and autumn. If you have sown its seed, it grows into the head, and delivers poorly in seed. If you set in a little head, it grows thin, and bears lots of seed. **Onions** want rich earth, vigorously dug over, watered, manured. There we'll make beds, cleaned of all weeds and rooting.

We'll sow on a calm clear day, especially when wind is from the
4   south-west or south-east. If they sow at the waning of the moon,

they come up thin and sharpish; if at the waxing, strong with a watery flavour. They are for setting in pretty thinly. Regular weeding and hoeing.

If we want their heads larger, we must remove all leaves. This way the juice will be forced down to the lower end.

Ones for gathering seed shall be helped with supports once they begin to shoot up stalk. When the seed colour is dark, they are showing the sign 'ripeness'. Young stems along with the seed need pulling off still half-dry, and drying like that in sun.

5   § This month you'll sow **dill**. Tolerates any weather conditions, but is happy when it's warmish. Shall be watered if the rain holds off. Shall sow pretty sparingly.

   NB Some don't bury its seed, thinking no bird will touch it.

§ Now, too, we can sow **mustard**.

§ This month too we'll sow **cabbage**, which can sow all the year round. Delights in rich soil, dug over sufficiently. Scared of potter's clay and gravel, doesn't fancy grit and sand, unless
6   running water comes to the rescue all through the year. **Cabbage** tolerates all weather conditions, by preference cold. They produce faster if put in to face south-west, late if north-facing – but the latter beats the field for flavour and strength of stalk. Delight in slopes, and for that reason seedlings are for putting in beds on raised 'cushions'. Enjoys dung and hoeing. Grows sturdy set out pretty scarcely.

Will quick cook and keep its greenness if while it has three or four leaves you sprinkle on top soda powder from a fine sieve, so it copies the way hoar frost looks.

7   **Columella** says[4] seedling roots are for wrapping in seaweed in order to keep the greenness, together with dung sticking to them. Seedlings with larger growth are for putting in because, though they take later, they'll grow stronger. If it's winter, the seedling needs setting on a warm day; if summer, when the sun goes down towards evening. It will grow huger if constantly buried with soil.

NB **Cabbage** seed turns to **turnip** with age.

8   This month after the Ides we'll start either to shape new **asparagus** 'sponges' from seed or else put in old ones. To me the method that seems cheap and thrifty is where we heap in one uncultivated or at least rocky spot lots and lots of **wild asparagus** root, to give fruit right away, from a spot that was supporting nothing.

We shall burn these too every year, in sprays, so the fruit comes right up more frequently and stronger. This variety has a more pleasant flavour.

9   § Now too **mallow** can sow.

§ Sow **mint** also, from seedling or roots, in a damp spot or around water. Wants sunny soil, neither rich nor manured.

§ This month you'll sow **fennel** at a sunny and moderately rocky spot.

§ At the beginning of spring **parsnip** sows. It will put out from seed and from seedling, in rich soil, loosened, deep trenched. You'll position it thin, to get it strength.

§ *'Cunila'* sows now as well, cultivation same style as **garlic** or **onion**.

§ Now **chervil** shall sow on cold spots, after the Ides. Wants land in good heart, damp and manured.

10   § This month we'll sow **beet**, though it can sow all summer. Loves crumbly land and a damp spot. For shifting when it has four or five leaves, roots smeared with fresh dung. Loves being dug up frequently and getting stuffed with lots of dung.

11   § This month **leek** for sowing. If you want **chives**, two months after it sows, you'll be able to cut it back without moving it from its bed – although **Columella** insists that even **chives** will last longer and better if shifted.[5] And every time it cuts, it shall be helped with water and dung.

If you want to have **leek**, with head, what you sow in spring you'll have to shift in October. It's to sow at a spot in good heart, especially on a plain, in a flat bed, deep-trenched, long dug over, well-manured. If you want **chives**, you sow thicker, if **leek**, thinner.

12 Needs frequent visits from the hoe, and freeing from weeds. When it has one inch thickness, it shall be shifted, leaves chopped off half way up and roots trimmed. Shall be smeared with liquid dung and separated four or five inches a time. When it gets roots, it needs grasping none too hard, and lifting with the hoe, so it hangs away from the earth, and is forced to fill up the empty space it finds below, with giant-size head. Likewise if you put in several seeds bound into one, a big **leek** will grow from all of them. Likewise if you stuck **turnip** seed on its head without using a blade, and set it in, it's said, there's a big increase in growth – better if you did this often.

13 § This month **elecampane** sows, where reed-beds are planted. Sows from 'eyes' like a cane. These we must snip off and lightly bury with earth, in dug and turned over soil, on raised 'cushions' laid along a line, on which the 'eyes' must dig in. They are separated by a three-foot spacing between them.

14 § This month we'll put in **Egyptian bean** bulbs. Love a damp spot, rich, specially well watered. Happy around springs and streams, and don't mind about soil quality, provided they are forever tended by moisture. They can almost make leaves for ever, if they are protected from cold with covering like citrus plantations.

§ This month **cummin** and **anise** sow at a well-dug spot, where you can mix in manure. What has been sown shall be cleaned of weeds continually.

(5) Month of March (4.9)

1 § Now is the best time for the garden to take up the start of cultivation.

§ In March **cardoon artichoke** sows. Adores manured and loosened earth, though it can come up better on rich soil. Can help counter moles if it is set in well-consolidated ground so the earth

2   isn't easy for these hostile creatures to tunnel. **Cardoons** are for sowing at the moon's waxing, in a pre-prepared bed, seed separated by half a foot's length.

> NB A precaution: seed must not be put in upside down, or they will breed them weak, bent over, and tough.

They are not for pressing in deep, but shall go down, in clutches of three fingers, until the earth reaches the first joint. Then they shall be lightly covered, continually freed of weeds until the

3   seedlings grow firm, and watered if a hot spell arrives. If you snapped the points of the seeds, they'll be prickle-free.

Likewise if you douse their seed for two days with oil of bay, **nard**, **balsam**, **rose**-sap, or mastic, and thereafter you dry and press them in, they will come up with the same flavour as the perfume the seeds drank in.

To be sure, every year the plants must be removed from the stock – so mother-plants don't get exhausted – and the young ones set out at different spacings. They are for pulling up together with a section of the root. The ones you keep for gathering seed, you'll need to free from all the shoots, and cover over with a sherd or bit of bark – the seed habitually dies of sun or rain.

4   NB To counter **moles** it does good to have cats often in the middle of artichoke-beds. Plenty of people have tame ferrets. Some fill mole holes with red clay or **wild cucumber** juice; quite a few open up a number of hollows beside the moles' nests, so they shy off in panic at their invasion by sun; the majority set snares at the entrance, with dangling mole bristles.

5   § This month too we'll sow well **wild garlic** and **garlic**, **onions**, *cunila*, on cold spots, and **dill**. Now **mustard** and **cabbage** sow or plant best, and **mallow** sows. **Wild radish** and **wild marjoram** seedlings shift. **Lettuce**, **beet**, and **caper** can sow, and **Egyptian bean** or **savory**, and **cress**. **Endive** too and **radish** sow now in some places, for use in summer.

6   § Now **melons** are for sowing, pretty thinly. Seed shall be two feet apart, on spots dug over or trenched, especially on sand. Its

seed is for soaking for two days in honeyed wine and milk; then dried and set in. From this they'll be sweetened, and, if their seed soaks for many a day in dry **rose**-leaves, they'll be scented.

7 § Now too **cucumbers** are seed sown thinly in furrows a foot and a half deep and three foot wide. Between furrows you leave an eight-foot space uncultivated, where they can ramble. They are helped by weeds, so they need no hoe or weeding.

If you soaked seed in sheep milk and honeyed wine, they'll grow sweet and white. They go long and tender if you put water in an open vessel under them, two palms width below – hurrying towards it is how they'll go.

8 They'll grow without sowing, if beforehand their seed is greased in Sabine oil, and rubbed in the herb called '*culex*' ['gnat'], in powder form. Some insert in a cane **cucumber** flower, along with the head of its cluster, first piercing all its knots. The **cucumber** grows there, stretching out real long.

> NB It so dreads olive oil that, if you plant it nearby, it curls up like a hook. Every time it thunders, it turns around as if in panic.

9 > NB If you enclose and fasten its flower, just as it is, on its tendril cluster, in a pottery mould, the sort of shape, man or beast, that it had, is produced in the shape of **cucumber**. All this laid down by Gargilius Martialis.[6]

Columella says,[7] on a sunny and manured spot, if we had brambles or fennel, after autumn equinox, these are cut close to the ground and hollowed out with a wooden spike, then we shove manure in among the 'marrow' core, and add cucumber seed – from this grow fruit that cannot be denied, even in cold snaps.

10 § This month we'll sow **asparagus** around 1 April in a rich spot, damp and dug as follows: two or three grains each shall be put in smallish grooves, set straight to a line, separated by a half-foot gap. Next the soil shall be covered with dung, and weeds be pulled up frequently, or through the winter straw be chucked on top, for removal at the start of spring. From this, **asparagus** will grow two years later.

Yet a less convoluted method is to put in **asparagus** 'sponges',
11 for delivering fruit fast. This is how they come: **asparagus** seeds,
as much as you could hold with three fingers, after the Ides of
February, at a rich, well-manured spot, you put in individual
ditches, and lightly bury. When they unite, there will grow an
intertwined root, known as a 'sponge'.

But this too involves a wait, as it is nourished through two years
in its seed-bed, with dung and constant weeding. Then it will
shift after autumn equinox, and in spring give **asparagus**. It
will be of more use to buy these, rather than nourish them with
long drawn-out suspense.

We'll set them out in furrows, though: if the spot is dry, in
mid furrow; if damp, on the top of the furrows. The moisture
must only water the **asparagus** 'sponges' on its way through,
not set on them.

12 The **asparagus** they produce first, we must snap off, not pull
away, so we don't move the still weak 'sponge'. Other years it
needs pulling so as to open the 'eyes' of the actual shoot, because,
if you snap them off successively, at a spot that used to be fertile,
they'll close if the **asparagus** root stays.

They'll deliver in spring, and in autumn you'll keep the one from
which you mean to take the seed. Afterwards you burns its sprigs,
then around winter you'll dress dung and ash on the 'sponges'.

13 § This month **rue** sows in sunny spots, satisfied with just a sprinkling of ash. It longs for a spot higher up, from which moisture
drains away.

If you put its seed in, still enclosed in mini-pouches, you'll have
to stick them in by hand, one by one. If they are already divided
up fine, you'll broadcast thin, rake them over, and cover them.
Those stalks that have grown from enclosed seed will be stronger
– but they'll grow late. Its sprays get pulled up in springtime,
along with a section of husk, and they will hold instead of
14 seedlings. A whole plant will die if shifted. Some insert its
shootlets in a holed bean or bulb, and bury them that way, to
be kept safe by energy from outside. They give them a send-off

with curses, even, and set them particularly in soil with loose brick, the surest thing for doing it good.

NB But as they insist, stolen **rue** will come up better.

NB It rests more happily under the shade of a fig tree. Begs that weeds be not dug out, but pulled up.

NB Scared stiff of the touch of an unclean woman.[8]

15 § From March through to the whole of October **coriander** sows. Loves rich earth, but grows even on thin soil. Seed which is getting old is thought better. Delights in moisture. Sown well, it will grow together with any veg. whatever.

16 § This month **gourd** is for sowing. Loves rich soil, damp, manured, loosened. A distinctive feature of **gourds** is that seeds which grow in their neck bear long thin ones; those which were in its belly make thicker **gourds**; those at the base, broad ones – if buried with tops downside up.

When they start to reach maturity, they shall be helped with supports. Ones kept for seed shall hang on their tendril cluster all through to winter, and then, once removed, set in the sun or smoke. Otherwise the seed rots, and perishes.

17 § This month **blite** spinach sows on any sort of soil – of culti-vated soil. This veg. is to be neither weeded nor hoed. Once it has grown, it will replenish itself through many generations by dropping its seed, so that, even if you wanted to, it could hardly be killed off.

§ Now too **wild thyme** sows, from seedlings or seed – improving with age. Will leaf more happily if sown beside a fish-pond, tank, or the edge of a well.

§ Also **anise** and **cummin** sow well now. Come up better at feel-good spots, and likewise other spots too, if helped with moisture and dung.

(6) Month of April (5.3)

1 § This month too is the last, now spring is pretty well past, that we can sow **cabbage**.

NB It will serve for stalk because it has lost the time for sprout.

§ Now **parsley** is well sown at hot and cold spots, any sort of soil, provided there is constant moisture there, though it won't refuse to grow even in dry conditions if need be. And it shall sow pretty well every month from the start of spring to the end of autumn.

2 From the same *genus*, is **horse parsley** – tougher, though, and more sour – and **marsh parsley** – soft leaf and tender stalk – which grows in tanks, and **rock parsley** – specially in rough spots. Hard-working people can have all these varieties.

You'll make **parsley** bigger if you wrap as much seed as can be held with three fingers with little strips of linen, and bury them in a shallow ditch. This way the growth of all the seeds will be linked by the solidity of a single head. They grow curly if the seeds are ground first, or if some weights roll over the growing beds, or they are heeled in as they emerge.

NB Older **parsley** seed grows quicker, new ones, later.

3 § This month we'll sow **orach**, if we can water it, in July or the rest of the months through autumn. Loves drenching with constant watering. Seed to be buried instantly on broadcasting. Greenery shall be plucked from it repeatedly. Though shifting is unnecessary when it sows well, yet it can grow up better if set in spaced out thinner, and helped by moisture – manure and water.

NB But it must be chopped back with a knife all the time, because this way *it doesn't stop sprouting*.

4 § Now **basil** sows. Said to grow fast if, the instant you've sown it, you spray it heavily with hot water.

NB Martialis[9] claims a marvel with basil: it produces blooms now purple, now white, now crimson, and if sowing from the seed is frequent, it changes now into **wild thyme**, now into **cat mint**.

5 § This month too **melons** and **cucumbers** sow, and **leek**, and at the start we'll put in **caper**, **wild thyme**, cuttings of

Egyptian bean, and sow **lettuce, beet, onion, coriander**, plus **endive**'s second sowing for summer use, and **gourds** and **mint** from root or seedling.

(7) Month of May (6.5)

§ The stretches of garden that are marked down for filling with seed in autumn, or seedlings, now will be the right time for **trenching**.

§ This month **parsley** is well sown, as already stated,[10] or **coriander, melons, gourds; artichoke, radish**, and **rue** will set in.

Leek seedling too shifts, for livening up with repeat watering.

(8) Month of June (7.4)

§ This month we'll sow **cabbage**, around the solstice, for shifting at the start of August, either in a watered spot or one sodden when rain gets going.

§ **Parsley** too we'll be able to sow successfully, **beet, radish, lettuce, coriander**, if we water them.

(9) Month of July (8.2)

1   § This month too we sow **onions** on watered or cool spots, and **radish** and **orach**, if we can water them, and **basil, mallow, beet, lettuce, leek** (to be watered).

§ This month on a watered spot we'll sow **navew** and **turnip** on crumbly, loose and non-dense spots. They are happy in damp spots and on plains, but **navew** grows better on dry, thinnish,
2   sloping, gravelly soil. Properties of the soil change both kinds of seed into the other: **turnip** sown on one soil for two years changes into **navew, navew** on another changes into **turnip**. They require well-dug, well-manured, turned-over soil, which will do plants and crops sown there the same year good. Four *sextarii*
3   of **turnip** are enough per *iugerum*, five of **navew**. If they are

119

dense, you'll thin them out so the rest grow sturdy. So that larger seeds will deliver, you dig out **turnips**, clean them of all the leaves, and you'll chop them down to a half-inch thickness at the stalk. Then you'll bury them in furrows carefully dug over, spaced eight inches apart, you chuck earth over them and heel it in. This way they'll grow large.

(10) Month of August (9.5)

1 § This month is also the last for sowing **turnip** and **navew** in dry spots – technique as stated.[11]

§ This month is the last that **radish** sow in drier spots, to serve up use in winter. Loves earth rich, loose, long dug over – like **turnip**. Dreads tufa and gravel. Enjoys cloud cover. For sowing with big gaps and deep digging. They come up better in sand.

2 They shall sow after fresh rainfall, unless they can be watered. What is sown must be covered over right away with a light hoe. At sowing, two *sextarii* will fill a *iugerum*, or, some say, four. No heaping on manure – even less, chaff, because from that they are pitted.

They grow sweeter if you sprayed them often with salt water.

> NB **Radishes** are thought to be female gender which are not so acid and have broader leaves, smooth and growing pleasurably green – so we gather seed from them.

3 They are believed to grow bigger if after all the leaves are removed, and the thin stalk sheds the soil, they get a frequent covering with earth.

If you would like them to grow sweet from sharp, you'll soak seed a day and a night in honeyed, or raisin, wine.

§ **Radish**, though, like **cabbage**, is agreed to be the vine's enemy. If they are sown around them, they shy away, so incompatible is the nature of them.[12]

§ This month too we'll sow **parsnips**.

(11) Month of September (10.13)

1   § Now **poppy** sows in dry hot spots. Can be seed sown together with other veg. It is said to come up more usable where twigs and shoots have been burned.

§ At this time you'll sow more usable **cabbage**, so that you can shift its seedlings at the start of November. They could produce **cabbage** in winter and **sprout** in spring.

2   § This month you'll need to **trench** three feet deep the stretches of garden that you are going to fill with seed through spring-time, and at the waning of the moon bring them manure.

§ This month is the last we'll sow **thyme** – yet it grows better from seedlings, though it could grow from seed too. Loves sunny, thin, coastal land.

§ Now around equinox you'll sow **wild marjoram**. Manuring and watering it welcomes, with open arms, till it grows strong. Loves rough and rocky spots.

§ In these days **caper** sows. Creeps far and wide, harms the earth with its sap – therefore to be sown, so it doesn't cover ground any further, with deeply dug soil surrounding it, or walls built tight of clay, on dry thin soil. Chases weeds of its own accord. Flowers in summer. **Caper** shrivels as the setting of the Pleiads draws on.[13]

3   § **Git** sows well in this its final month. We'll sow **cress** this month, and **dill**, in moderate and hot spots, **radish** in dry spots, with **parsnips** and **chervil**, around 1 October, with **lettuce**, **beet, coriander**, and in the first days **radish** and **navew**.

(12) Month of October (11.11)

1   § In the month of October **endive** is for sowing, to service winter. They love damp and loose soil. On sand, salty spots, and the coastline, the cream of them come up.

A pretty flat bed shall be readied for them, so their bare roots aren't exposed as the earth slips off. Plants with four leaves shall shift to a well-manured spot.

§ Now seedlings of **artichoke** are put in. When we put them in, we shall cut back the top of their roots with a knife, and we dip them in dung. We space them three-foot lengths apart, or when put down in a one-foot ditch to promote growth, two- or three-foot lengths. Often on dry days as winter draws on, we'll mix in ash and dung.

2   § This month we'll sow **mustard**. Loves ploughed soil and, if possible, banked-up earth, although it grows anywhere and everywhere. Needs hoeing often, so it can get a sprinkling of the dust that nourishes it: it doesn't like too much moisture.

One which you are setting out for gathering seed from, you'll leave be in its original spot. One you'll be preparing for food, you'll make stouter by shifting.

With **mustard**, old seed is useless, whether for sowing or for use. Break one with the teeth and, if it seems green inside, it is new; if it's white, that is a confession of age.

3   § This month **mallow** is for sowing – it will be checked from growing to any length by winter's onset. Loves manure.

Its seedlings shift when they start to have four leaves or five. The seedling of it that is tender takes better. Shifted bigger, it will flop. Their flavour is better if *not* shifted. But to stop them quickly lifting into stalk, you'll place in their middle little clods or pebbles. Needs setting thin. Delights in the hoe constantly. They are for freeing from weeds in such a way that they don't feel movement in the root.

> NB If you would make a knot in the root when shifting seedlings, they will grow squat.

4   § Now too in moderate and hot spots we'll sow **dill**. **Onions** sow this month, too, plus **mint** and **parsnip**; **thyme** and **wild marjoram** and **caper** at the start of the month. Ditto **beet** in drier spots.

We'll also sow '*armoracia*' or shift it to cultivated ground so it grows better – it is a **radish** that is **wild**.

5 § Now we must shift **leek** sown in springtime, so it grows at the head. To be sure it shall be dug all round constantly with the hoe, and the **leek** seedling will be grabbed and raised, as if with a claw, so the empty space which will underlie the roots fills up with growth of head.

§ **Basil** too we'll sow just now – it is said, it grows faster at this time if a light dousing sprinkles on a vinegar shower.

(13) Month of November (12.6)

§ This month **garlic** sows well, and **wild garlic**, on earth as white as possible, trenched and dug over, but *no* dung. You'll make drills in the beds and put seed in the higher-up spots, four inches apart, and pressed in no deeper. You'll hoe often, and so they'll grow more.

If you want to make it head, when the stalk starts to come out, tread it in. This way the sap will return to the spikes.

> NB It is said, if sowing is when the moon is underground, and pulling up is when the moon is likewise lurking underground, its smell will be stench free.

Garlic stored in chaff or hung in smoke will last.

§ Now too **onion** can sow, and **artichoke** seedlings be set out, and **wild radish** and '*cunila*' sow.

(14) Month of December (13.3)

§ At this time **lettuce** to sow, so its seedling shifts in February.

§ Also now **garlic, wild garlic, onions, mustard,** '*cunila*' will be sowable, following the lesson and method already recounted.[14]

Plate 8 Detail of a large mosaic pavement from the north-east portico of the Great Palace of the Emperors, Constantinople. *C.* 500–550 CE. A detail taken from Walker Trust Album, Baxter papers: MS36966A.

NOTES

Tying up loose ends

INTRODUCTION: RESERVING A PLOT

1 If this means roses could be grown there (in Lucania, south Italy) for spring and for autumn, it's unstartling; if the same plant bloomed in both seasons, it's a marvel in the pursuit of paradise. Virgil waves it at us as his sampler for all we are missing from him; as such, it is much-quoted by later writers (usually minus the 'twice cropping' (e.g. C.10.37). In terms of poetics, it speaks to the text and topic as a paradisal double-act. And it is a bridge, too, since Roman 'rose-beds' flower on the farm, although roses did grow in the garden.

2 Throughout, *intibum* will be translated into English as the inevitable, etymological, and traditional 'endive': but experts such as Jacques André are sure the plant is our 'chicory' (see *Further Reading: General*).

3 The sample of the garden we must imagine (write) for ourselves begins with mythic geography as the poet bids to memorialize the classical tradition of the garden of poetry: Oebalus (a founding father, cf. Chapter 2, n. 24 below) and Galaesus (*black* 'River *of Milk*'?) specify Tarentum. The Old Gardener is allusively named after a poetic cave of inspiration on Mt Parnassus. See Preface.

4 Virgil has now put the garden onto the farm, where it belongs, in a corner. See Preface. The ancient commentary on Virgil tells us that Q. Gargilius Martialis was the one to step into this breach (Servius' note on V.G.4.147–8. See Maire (2002) in *Further Reading: General*.): Columella *would* be peeved, after all his hard work in following Virgil's instructions (10 *Preface* 3).

CHAPTER 1: PRODUCE IN PROSE

1 *Claudius*, priest in the cult of the divinised emperor Augustus, sounds like the right sort of modest force for 'clos-ure' that a garden requires in order to be a garden, and a textual cameo (meaning 'enclosure': C.10.28, *claud-atur*). *Augustalis* hints at 'increase' (*augeo*), the hallowed aim of the Roman farm: Book 11 grows the work bigger, moving beyond the 'bonus' of Book 10, and appearing to claim the role of closure for itself. (Book 12 will come as *another* complete surprise: cuisine. See Preface.)

2 C.'s unknown addressee, P. Silvinus, bears a 'significant name' – culture clears *woodland* (*silua*) into farm, works raw nature into cultivated art.

3 C.11.2 and 11.3.

4 1.8.1–14.

5 Quoting V.*G*.4.133, of the 'Corycian old-timer'.

6 Democritus (fifth century BCE) heads C.'s list of philosophers who helped farming after Hesiod broke the ice: 'springing up from the sources of wisdom' (1.1.7). All sorts of manuals later traded more or less brazenly/openly under his name. Only Columella cites his lost *Georgics* (three times), and only this citation comes close to a quote (in translation).

7 The *Ides* was the heart of the Roman month, its central divide (in March, May, July, October the Ides fell on the 15th; in other months on the 13th). A favourite growing marker because, as Columella intones, from the launchpad of 13 January (11.2.4): 'Half a month too early is none too early, half a month late isn't late' – when it's a question of getting jobs done within the flexi-time constraints of the weather.

8 23–30 August.

9 *Apium* (etymologized as 'bee-plant') covers *both* our parsley *and* our celery: *this* chapter is about celery. Intolerable terminology for *us* to cope with.

10 23–30 August.

11 C.9.4.6: thyme is best, wild thyme second best, *cunila* third-rate.

12 23–30 August.

13 Emperor of Rome, 14–37.

14 C. calls Bolus ghost-writer of pseudo-Democritus' (lost) *Manufacture* (7.5.17). Vitruvius (*On Architecture* 9.1.14) and Pliny (24.160) accept it as genuine Democritus. We are told that Bolus was a Pythagorean philosopher – historian, writer on marvels, theoretical physicist, meteorologist (Suda, entry under his name).

15 19–23 March.

16 See above, n. 6.

17 C. refers to C. Iulius Hyginus, late first-century BCE former slave, and librarian, of the emperor Augustus, eleven times – seven on bees, where he is 'the hardest-working' authority (9.2.1). He wrote *On Farming, Bees, Vines and Orchards, Roman Precedents, The Trojan Families, Roman Religion, Cities of Italy, Commentaries on Virgil* (all lost).

18 See above, nn 6, 14.

19 For this 'List of Contents', see Preface.

CHAPTER 2: FLOWERY VERSE

1 See Chapter 1, n. 2 above, for P. Silvinus.

2 Virgil, at *G*.4.147–8, above. Columella has worked into ambitiously powerful prose all that tradition reprocessed through experience taught him of farming. Now he will try to 'remember' everything that Virgil, by gesturing towards the garden he would not write, intimated about the difference that poetry made to all of his farm. That is, he will *not* 'do a Virgil', in the sense that Columella's farm is *un*poetic, but he *will*, in that he lets the aura of *the* Roman Poet instruct and inform his own attempt to capture gardening for *his* book, in the dual role of celebration of the joys of the good life, and pleasure of the text. By writing on, and reconverting to his prose (books 11–12), Columella will provide his own intimations of 'precepts' for approximating paradise, arising from his own visit to Virgil's farm, and Virgil's garden. But he will pass them on to us transmuted by his own living through their blessings – and their shortcomings.

3 A no-nonsense *Greek* proverb (*Corpus Paroemiographorum Graecorum* 1.270, n. on Diogenian 6.4), just at the point where this no-nonsense Roman expert flips into excited frenzy. Columella both belittles gardening and singles it out as the gem that encapsulates existence. It stands in for the whole range of applied creativity that materializes in every *un*glamorous, perhaps unglamorizable, operation down on the farm. In short, Garden *supplements* Farm – sums it up, as recap, and completes it (realizes it fully, brings it to fruition), as 'bonus'. Gardeners *don't* talk their garden patches up.

4 For Silvinus, see C.10 *Preface* 4.

5 As signalled in the Preface, Columella pins his *Gardening* to Virgil's 'blank page, with instructions' left for posterity to imagine. Columella's phrases here paraphrase keynote wording taken from the opening programme of V.*G.*, and from its resumptions at the head of each book (e.g. *Pales*, Roman goddess of pasturage, is from V.*G.*3.1). Columella's first words, 'Horticulture, too, . . . you', hit the nail on the head, but at the same time manage to quote Virgil (V.*G.*4.118), and to rejig his formula for bolting on the second half of your poem ('You, too . . .', V.*G.*3.1). Columella's start, 'First move, a home' (v. 8), also quotes Virgil's start for V.*G.*4, so we will not miss that *his* garden of verse means to live up to the master's finale, exploding the tangential evocation into a whole brash book of technicolour stunts by the myriad – 'A garden symphony'.

6 Most of Columella's choice of 'soil' naturally parades the text and texture of Virgil's *Georgics* (thanks to Virgil, and in his honour, Columella makes the frogs' 'ancient complaint' of V.*G.*1.378 'eternal'); but blood-'red elderberries' grew in Virgil's pastoral poetry, the *Eclogues* (10.27: see n. 10 below).

7 Columella's plot starts rough. Wild and weird herbage-verbiage with no place in poetry needs sorting from phrases with potential for his garden (from Virgil's *Georgics*). The 'Christ's thorn's spines so sharp' take us back to Virgil's *Eclogues* (5.38): Columella pegs his *Garden* close to those songs from herdsmen resting in the shade – closer, ultimately, than to Virgil's *Georgics*? (See n. 10 below.)

8 Columella parades great names from the mythology and canon of 'Greek Sculpture' – as rejected models for the artist of his garden. His plot wants for its icon an art(ist)-less wooden scarecrow, the fertility god Priapus. All grotesque (?) erection and razor-sharp (?) pruning-hook ('sickle'), he is ready to assault and castrate all unwanted visitors up the garden path. Here is the core of Columella's topiary, where no genius or ego creams the credit that belongs to tradition, belongs to the *un*sublime pieties of *gardening*.

9 Now he has chosen a plot, fixed a source to supply water, and centred his tutelary deity, Columella is ready to start up, for real. He works citation of Virgil's first item of gardening (V.*G.*4.119, above) into a second run of phrases grafted from Virgil's introductory litany of the topics programmed for his whole poem, at the very start of V.*G.*1. Set – 'by Virgil' – to turn the *Georgics* inside-out, C.10 is on its way, a marginal sketch amplified to score a concerto.

10 A metaphor of producing text as 'spinning thread' adapts for the garden here to 'channelling water'. Columella wants classical poetry to irrigate his gardening, fetching inspiration all the way from the primal Greek source of Hesiod's farming poem, *Works and Days* (*Pierides*, v. 1), through the refining channels of later Greek poetry, to feed the Roman countryside of Virgil's work. (C.10's last line will remind us that V.*G.* reminded us that it sang Hesiod's song; see below, n. 62.) Now the

tradition feeds Columella, he derives direct inspiration here, not from Virgil's *Georgics*, but from *his* first poems, the *Eclogues* (reworking 6.5) – small-scale pastoral paradise, at least in comparison with the farming to come.

11 Columella will tip poetry all over the time that governs life in the garden text. Connecting plants and their cultivation to the workings of the cosmos, he beefs up the myth, and proves that gardening always was as grand a theme as any epic thundering: he will tuck it all away again in Book 11. 'Sirius sets' at 'the autumn equinox' occurring on 24–26 September. 'Autumn' is a personification, rather than a deity.

12 This pair of astronomical flourishes takes Virgil's lead (V.G.1.221–2: also quoted at C.2.8.1), but pumps up the eroticism to fill his garden with atmosphere. Bacchus' love was Ariadne, now the constellation of the Northern Crown: she sets on 9 November. 'Atlas' daughters' are the Pleiads, their morning setting on 8 November.

13 On the stargazer's calendar, Phoebus, the sun god who just scared the Pleiads from the sky, now crosses from Scorpio to Sagittarius on 18 November. The gardener's sky is full of dangerous vermin, strange monsters come to the rescue, and we are heading for the first salvo from Columella's arsenal of almighty shocks in making gardening weird, wonderful, and –

14 – primeval. Here in dead of winter, Columella takes up another early motif from V.G. (1.62–3), to picture the gardener's first tangle with work as a horrible mutilation of our mother, Earth. Only, Columella raises the spectre so as to banish its nightmare. For his play with the 'logic' of Greek Myth here, see Preface.

15 Columella could do with readers used to rude awakenings from didactic poetry – who remember how Virgil broke the ice by shunting from cosmogonic scenery to getting the trainee farmer on parade, ready to roll up the sleeves, and dig in (V.G.1.62–3). Latin naturally and normally gives Earth, and all her little plant babes, 'hair' all over the garden/poem, where English plants only get 'tresses' in rotten translationese like mine. Will foliage as 'clothing' work any better?

16 'Warm' is a graphic emendation doubted by editors tepid, lukewarm, through cool. The text of C.10 generates remarkably few disputes (cf. just n. 29 below, on v. 130).

17 This hysterical gang-rape and -torture by the winds is the poet whipping up lashings of electric energy in 'epic storm' style so as to launch a book of melodrama, and release an onslaught of – petals. See Preface.

18 'Riphaea' means a wild arctic (mountain), 'Zephyr' a thawing spring (breeze. Virgilian: V.G.4.518; 1.44). C.11.2.15 keys the west wind's coming on 7 February.

19 The Lyre constellation sets on 1–3 February. For the dung, cf. farmer Virgil to *his* ploughboys: V.G.1.80.

20 C.11.2.21 specifies the first swallow for 20 February. Quaint, pious, charming, ludicrous . . .

21 This Greek flower gets a Latin gloss, 'white uns'.

22 Latin's 'wild lion' is most likely our antirrhinum.

23 Megara is in central Greece, Sicca in North Africa (*Gaetulia*).

24 Rocket, surefire aphrodisiac, keeps the erotic tension ticking over outside the kitchen window.

25 C. promotes 'Syrian root/radish' to 'A*s*syrian' for fun; Pelusium was in the Nile delta: wine was the life for Greeks and Romans, not barbeerian beer. Fennel is 'menacing' because used for caning children (the second meaning at 10.21).

26 This is Athena's olive oil, the best from her Athens backyard.

27 *Lepidium* is here derived from the Greek *lepizo*, peel. The way, apparently, you get rid of that tattoo.

28 Columella's Ode to Cabbage gives us a tour of central and southern Italy and back again, in fifteen preciously minute rows of words: cf. Preface. 'Parthenope' is Naples, 'city of culture', where Virgil says he wrote *Georgics* (V.G.4.564), and its flowery phrase is a cultured mock-quote from Virgil's final work, the great epic of empire, where a certain *Oebalus* will 'not go unsung by the poet's song' – he is *son* of 'Sebethus' girl' (*Aeneid* 7.734). The places meant lots in the growth of Rome, but Pompeii and Herculaneum detain us by accident – the accident that buried them not twenty years after Columella stopped writing. The 'leek' at the end of the paragraph that began by not bothering to name its theme, 'cabbage', is a red herring, for fun. ('Mother Aricia' quotes a second time from the *Aeneid* catalogue of Italian braves, where her child was weird Virbius, no onion, 7.762.)

29 'Slime' (or 'swamp') is one manuscript reading here; 'turf' is another.

30 Aries' rising occurs on 23 March. This is the 'Golden Fleece' story, with two children persecuted by a step-mother, just like something out of a Roman Caesar's Golden Palace . . . Mother Earth is about to hug everything in the garden, whether 'hers' (seed sown in her) or 'fostered' (shifted seedlings planted in her). In the Greek Myth, oceans of epic and tragedy start here; Columella winds up to a tumble of lovely veg.

31 Terminology for parsnip and carrot intertwines thoroughly: the expert Jacques André insists that classical *pastinacae* are pretty well all carrots (and *siser* is our parsnip. See *Further Reading: General*).

32 Mt Hybla in Sicily spells honey and pastoral, Canopus in Egypt means Alexandrian scholarship and incest. Luscious cicely imported from Greece out-scents the poets' favourite story of Cinyras' incest with daughter Myrrh(a). Hyacinths grew from Ajax's blood.

33 Some form of cabbage, in antithesis with healthy lettuce, the Greek name *cor-amble* is probably etymologized ('eye-blunter'): at 175, Greek *amaranths* were glossed as 'not-withering'.

34 Columella's lettuces include types from all over the Roman world, and the Roman archive: two sorts named after a great Republican general; one from out east in Anatolia, at one end of the earth (Cappadocia), one from Columella's home town, Cadiz (Gades), at the other. Cypriot Paphian sounds sexy already (see after 193).

35 Months twin with types of lettuce: the sun is in Aquarius in January; February (once the fag-end of the Roman year) hosted rites for the dead (Feralia), and fertility rites that came to drag in Pan (as Lupercus, the Lupercalia); Mars' month is March, paired with Venus' April (she had a major cult at Paphos on Cyprus).

36 Ocean and Neptune impregnate their wives and equally the sea teems with life. Jupiter rides again, playing the shower of rain trick he once used on Danae in myth – but this time he comes down, not on some (Acrisius') locked-up daughter, but on . . . Mother Earth.

37 Columella sounds like a crazed version of the Roman poet Lucretius, see Preface (for *mater terra* = *materia*). Columella will now get back to work – figured as pruning and gardening (10.228–9). From his reverie from Delphi, on a Dionysiac freak-out past the Mother Goddess Cybele's home in Anatolia, following Dionysus' vertiginous route all the way from his birthplace in Nysa, way out east, to triumph over the city of Thebes, beneath Mt Cithaeron, take his rightful place beside Apollo at

Delphi, and have his half of the 'Pierian, Parnassian' action of the Muses. Infusing Dionysus builds the voice of praise into a howl of delight, sub-linguistic cries for Apollo 'Paean of Delos', and Dionysus 'Paean of [yelps of adoration]'.

38 The spray of phrases through vv. 237–41 *may* instead read as a run through the phases of the development.

39 The 'Punic tree' is the pomegranate (*punic* meant red in Greek). 'Dragon root' is one sort of *arum*. Coriander is famous for stinking. Black cummin and fennel flower combine to make good seasoning.

40 The wild lion/snap dragon/antirrhinum (or 'bunny-rabbit'), again (v. 99).

41 Spring returns for a second gasping display of high-octane thrill. The flowers are ready to pick. Eyes open, jaw drops, girls blush, perfume as good as the Queen of Sheba's. Muses are girls, whichever way you look at it (here they are named for the myth where Pegasus' hoof struck their pool of inspiration on Mt Helicon). Thus they are sisters – sisters to all the long list of sisters that throng the erotic land-scapes of classical poetry. Including the friends of Ceres' daughter Proserpine, out flower-picking in Sicily (near Enna) when the god of Hell surfaced to pick a bride (in Ovid's great epic of myth (and sex), *Metamorphoses* 5.552). She was kidnapped, raped, wed, and enthroned. Her mother gets her back, then loses her, annually. And that is our year, our seasons. Columella tries it on his chosen nymphs, all over again: 'Trust me, gentle maidens, you are safe with me' . . .

42 Garden flowers belong to Dione's daughter: Venus . . . Girls, Muses, flowers, poetry, they all spell sex: 'Sarra' is a way not to say 'Tyre', where purple dye (and women like Queen Dido . . .?) originated. Leto's daughter 'Phoebe' is the eternal virgin Diana. 'Sirius' and 'Fire star' (planet Mars) are a summer on heat. 'Evening/Morning Star' frame an all-nighter. Thaumas' daughter Iris is a rainbow of flowers, on legs. Mother Earth's eye runs approvingly over these beds full of ripe blooms.

43 Up at dawn to pick the buds, Columella goes back to (reawaken) what may be Virgil's earliest poem (*Eclogue* 2.18–19, 45–55; v. 299 adapting, and out-grossing, ibid. 5.44), where goatherd Corydon despairs of beloved Alexis' scorn. Another wild nymph, their 'Naiad', can come to fetch more baskets of flowers, to help Virgil's poem win the day, repair the (w)hole in his poetry, and . . . ultimately make an old peasant a very happy man, safe behind a Virgilian hedge: v. 310 has Columella's flower garden bringing back a sell-out profit just like the cheese of Virgil's Tityrus, who lives on, to sing and play pastoral through his sunset years – the prototype of the *Georgics*' 'Corycian old-timer' (*Eclogue* 1.33–6).

44 Vertumnus is another 'Priapus' figure, humble peasant god of produce, and produc-tivity – of spring (*uer*), of the turning seasons (*uerto*), of verse (*uersus*).

45 The Sun crosses into Gemini on 19 May; into Cancer on 19 June. (Cancer became a star when Hercules killed the crab sent to get him with poison from Hercules' victim, the Hydra from Lerna. Does the Sun god enjoy gobbling crab claws?)

46 The Roman deity *Fors Fortuna* had her festival on 24 June.

47 Columella announces a pot-pourri of mumbo-jumbo. Roman religion called many of its peculiar ways 'Etruscan'. The blight, 'rust', had its own 'goddess' and festival, featuring . . . dead puppy-dog (the *Robigalia*, for *Robigo*) on 25 April. Tages and Tarchon are fine, fun, masks for Columella to wear for an atavistic moment (why, oh why, an Arcadian ass skull, you ask? Well, right through Roman antiquity, 'Arcadian asses' were 'the original imports – big and tall', the seventh-century linguistic cosmologist and Bishop of Seville tells us: Isidore, *Etymologies* 12.1.40;

cf., from a millennium of classical Latin earlier, Plautus, *Asinaria* 333. I hope that will do. But: white bryony – against the Almighty, you gasp? Don't. On this one, I can't help you). Then Columella hops right into Greek myth, courtesy of Virgil, whose 'teachers, centaur Chiron and Melampus son of Amythaon' *fail* to stop the farmer's hell of cattle plague, as he steams towards his last, redemptive, book (V.*G*.3.550). Columella's garden isn't invulnerable, but it's one hell of a lot safer than out there on the wide open farm.

48 Dardanus is another wizard. Columella makes him *sound* like a founder of 'Dardanian' Troy, mythic origin of Rome. The crediting of this throwback stuff about menstruating 'heifers' to Dardanus may be down to pseudo-Democritus, 'pupil of Dardanus' (P.30.9).

49 The Greek *kampe* (meaning 'bendy'?) is mock-glossed in Latin here.

50 The Golden Fleece story has moved on. Jason and the Argonauts, from Iolcos in Thessaly, pass all the tests, and recover the Fleece from its dragon-serpent guard, thanks to the potions of the infatuated virgin Medea – menstruating or not.

51 Those lettuces, from Columella's town, and from Venus', make an unbeatable combination (vv. 193–4).

52 Columella shows how versatile (his) gourds can be (like his poetry): Narycus: in south – 'Greek' – Italy, or Mt Hymettus overlooking Athens; like water, or wine. (And, anywhere there's a river, and kids, you need . . . waterwings.)

53 Greek myth's Erigone became the constellation Virgo, and her dog became Sirius. The Sun god (*Hyperion*) crosses into Virgo on 20 August.

54 This is an astonishing story (myth) about how any wonderful exotic import – a peach, a potato, tomato, genetic modification – *could* always be the doom of us all (cf. discussion in P.15.45).

55 Arcturus rises and sets on 5 and 17 September.

56 Columella will not lower himself to name 'figs' (again – see C.5.9–11, where an overlapping, but different 'top ten' varieties spill out): the types blend 'Livian', allegedly named somehow after the first empress of Rome, Livia, wife of Augustus, with 'Libyan' and 'Lydian'; and plenty of alliterative Greek varieties in between. It is a generous list, and it turns out to be The End.

57 Volcanalia on 23–30 August. The end is nigh.

58 In Virgil's epic, 'Nursia sent' warriors, not turnips (*Aeneid* 7.715). *Bunias* may, or may not, just be Greek for navew. (Amiternum is in central Italy, near Naples: home of plenty of produce, as we shall learn.)

59 You can feel the wave of ecstasy building here, as Columella's vintage is due, praise be to . . . [that yelp of adoration], Dionysus. Full circle, The End.

60 Satyrs and Pans are subordinate aspects of Dionysus – bestial/masculine – always dancing on the edge, and acclaimed as Arcadian (after Mt Maenalus), as liberating (*Lyaeus*), and wine-pressing (*Lenaean*). Invoking, and outbidding, for this closing ceremony of *The Garden*, the *opening* invocation of V.*G*.2, the book on viticulture (vv. 2, 4–8). The vintage festival in the Roman calendar was the Vinalia Rustica (on 19 August).

61 See Chapter 1, n. 2 above, for P. Silvinus.

62 Columella cites Virgil's evaluation of *his* avatar, Hesiod of Ascra (V.*G*.2. 175–6). In the *Book of Gardening*, 'unbarring the old sources' speaks directly to the poetics of 'irrigation' (cf. n. 10 above).

CHAPTER 3: NATURE'S MIRACLES

1 These topics filled Book 18.201–365.
2 Flax will take up Book 19.1–26. Esparto, truffles and such, silphium and the like, madder (for dye), 'radicula' (soapwort? for cleaning cloth white) will bridge to The Garden (19.27–48).
3 Pliny plays at the big build-up for the new topic. Fetching the apple guarded by the Hesperides nymphs (somewhere in mythic Africa) was one of the Labours of Hercules; the so-called Gardens of Adonis were an exotic Greek women's 'summer lust' ritual, which featured lamenting pot plants with forced life-expectancy; Alcinous' garden stars as paradise in the archetypal 'backyard' epic, Homer's Odyssey; Pliny does not come back in Natural History to the Hanging Gardens – whether Queen's or King's.
4 Pliny will return, less enigmatically, to Tarquin and the Riddle of the Poppies: below, 19.169.
5 After Greek and Roman myth, Pliny turns to Latin lexicography – another medium for myth piously passed down from book to book.
6 Next, a couple of myths in the field of Roman religion: both items are grist to Pliny's mill, as he gets past the foil (the flannel) of vestiges of antiquity, and tips over into the juicy decline and fall into the present.
7 We have a score of Plautus' comedies from the early second century BCE, but no such reference survives.
8 Blame the Greeks, their philosophy, their hedonism, for our topsy-turvy world, our perverted language: Pliny does! Early third-century BCE Epicurus made teaching 'in the garden' his slogan for the pursuit of paradise – and pleasure infected the planet?
9 Now Pliny does what he does loudest – berates his Rome's superpower expansion for destroying Roman solidarity, integrity, morality, community, society, you-name-ity.
10 Those oysters spelled pearls. 'Phasis birds' (pheasant) bring with them Medea's mythical witchery-pokery and deadly poison, all the way from Colchis out east. 'Numidian birds' (guinea fowl) are flown in from North Africa. 'Ethiopian birds' (ruffs?) in myth periodically flock there to the tomb of King Memnon, and . . . Pliny has seen them on the plate at Rome? Huh – he knows he's banging the same old drum (he is about to tell us so).
11 Sociology of bread: see P.18.87, 105–6.
12 Pliny here wheels out the obsolete 'tribes', electoral divisions of the Roman citizens. Time melts away as his voice booms like a censor from the Republic of yore. Heritage culture.
13 The bettering of asparagus fails to sound so very bad, and these 'thistles' were the stock from which artichokes would breed.
14 With the traditional sang froid, our censor now admits the old days were riven, too (the early Republic saw the people walk out on their nobles, for one sanctuary or stronghold after another). Pre-communal Rome is the custom-made lesson to spank post-communal Rome with.
15 Only a mad bad emperor like Gaius (Caligula, 37–41) would try slapping tax on Roman food. Pliny either expects his clue-less reference to be obvious or doesn't mind us floundering.
16 Pliny is by now asphyxiated by his own rhetorical strain. The tirade has become wonderfully silly – time to bail, or bale, out.

17 Cato, *Farming* 156.1, sprouting into a veritable Ode to Cabbage as the wonder aid for digestion (156–7). At last, Pliny lets the Cato out of the bag: the early second-century BCE Elder Cato had famously made the censorial voice of Roman Republican oratory his own. And *he* had written Roman farming into the archive (cf. 93, 136, 145, 147, below; cf. Gratwick (2002) in *Further Reading: General.*). The Garden feeds Pliny's Cato habit, and he mixes up another lovely Roman bowlful of peasant nostalgia – those 'salad days' when men were men, and cabbage was king . . . (The bite about the bad housewife is a fair old impersonation of Cato, not the real thing, unless this mouthful has got lost from our texts of his *Farming*.)

18 'Salad' is *'acetaria'*, which *says* 'vinegary-stuff'. (And *'salad'*? Salad = 'Salted (herbage)', so they say.)

19 Inner-city decay and deprivation at its worst? Pliny enjoyed dreaming up this vista – the denial of every Roman's right to a window-box, the disappearance of the burglarized population behind barricades boxing in their every window . . . (see Linderski (2001): see *Further Reading: General*).

20 If you put in effort and caring on a Plinian scale, you can dig up *one* Valerius *Lactucinus*: the totally obscure M. Valerius Lactucinus Maximus, son of the obscure fifth-century BCE consul M. Valerius Lactuca, a generation after the quaestor M. Valerius Maximus Lactuca. I *did* say: those were the (salad) days, when mighty magistrates were Lettuces, and lettuce was The Greatest.

21 Lettuce, pray: Virgil *does* start up his final onslaught on *Farming* with the come-on: 'The effort is on a paper-thin topic' (V.*G*.4.6). But do try to keep up, and put in effort and caring on a Pliny scale: Virgil was going to hive off gardening from coverage, making a bee-line instead for the apiary. He did not 'confess' to any manufacturing 'difficulties', or even brag of the challenges, of (bee-)keeping bathos out of mock-heroics on minibeasts. No, Virgil's line continues: 'But – '. And Pliny expects us to know this: 'But the glory is *not* paper-thin. . .'. It shouldn't bug us if Pliny does misbehive for an instant, as he takes us into his garden: his stinging sermon trumpets the palpable 'effort and caring he really has put in' to plant research. His garden of drugs isn't Virgil's pipe-dream, but it deserves 'to meet with plinny of appreciation'.

22 Pliny's rage for order will work this 'product-based' sorting through many a distraction. But the classifying regularly keeps the gardening safe, not down. 'Gristle' (or 'cartilage') drops out of modern botany, but it is a master-category for Pliny: 'above ground' = cucumber and gourd (19.64–74); 'below ground' = navew, turnip, radish; 'woodier' = parsnip/carrot, marsh-mallow, rampion, elecampane (75–92).

23 For the Hesperides, see above, n. 3. Pliny told us of Lixus in Mauretania at 5.3–4. (An Altar of Hercules celebrated another of his Labours.) These mythic trees are beyond anyone wrapping their minds around.

24 *Fungi*: scarcely touched on (P.16.31, cf. 19.38); truffles: P.19.33–7.

25 Tiberius, emperor of Rome 14–37.

26 Beside the lower Danube, at the fighting front of the Roman Empire.

27 Someone has just talked Pliny up the garden path and over the garden wall. He's in too much of a lather to see it, but these ripe 'facts' he harvests from whatever book comes his way leave *their* stalks behind. Or else Pliny knows exactly how to get gardening readers on their mettle – and fascinated. Every time he mentions another 'wonder' or 'marvel', we know we are being manipulated, whether pandered to or toyed with.

28 C.11.3.53, above.

29 This is from the great fourth-century BCE philosopher, naturalist, and systematizer Theophrastus: *Plant Research* 7.4.6. P.19 relies on him most of all: but the tangled undergrowth of notelets ahead shows no allegiance to him or to anyone else: 'No book ever was so bad that somewhere in it isn't usable' was Pliny's mantra (The Younger Pliny, *Letters* 3.5.10).

30 21 April.

31 19–23 March.

32 P.20.11–17.

33 P.18.126–32.

34 Navews/turnips ('*neeps*' and '*tur-neeps*') and radishes get mixed up left-right, and centre, in and between both Greek and Roman/Latin languages and cultures. Worse is on its way here: see below, nn 35, 47, 76.

35 Close rendering of Theophrastus, *Plant Research* 7.4.2 (but on *radishes*).

36 Both sorts from the hills of central Italy (Amiternum: C.10.422, P.18.130).

37 P.18.131–2.

38 See n. 76 below, for a surprise – a blight on Pliny's gardening.

39 A peak close to Rome.

40 C.11.3.16 and 59 does have a 'Syrian root (or radish)'.

41 Pliny is an expert on Germany, real and written. His fighting and writing careers both began there: see Preface, p. 21.

42 23–30 August.

43 P.1.11 cites the *c.* third- to first-century BCE Aristomachus' lost *On Apiculture*; P.14.120 probably notes his lost *Wine to Keep*.

44 Cf. P.11.114 for this lousy disease, which has not survived antiquity.

45 A proud 'Catonian' story of a real Roman (Cicero, *On Old Age or Cato Maior* 55, Plutarch, *Life of Cato* 2). Was Manius Curius *Dentatus* ('Big Teeth') named for that turnip, or is the nickname where the story came from? (See Pliny's next note but one!)

46 This mid-first-century medical writer is a great loss – on cabbage and cosmetics, too.

47 This may be a slip by Pliny (as you may know, vines usually panic at *cabbages*). When Pall. 9.5.3, below, names *both* radish *and* cabbage in the role, it may be down to systemic poisoning by Pliny.

48 Cf. Chapter 1, n. 17.

49 P.25.110–12. Remember that all these 'parsnips' are most probably 'carrots' instead: Chapter 2, n. 31.

50 Like Pliny, Tiberius, emperor of Rome 14–37, spent years fighting on the Rhine front ('*Gelduba*' is Gelb, near Düsseldorf).

51 This became the title of Livia as Augustus' widow (priestess, and 'adoptive daughter': 58 BCE–29). On something of a health-kick, she lived to be 86 (cf. P.14.60).

52 Cato, *Farming* 8.2. Were these 'Megara bulbs' *really* grape hyacinths?

53 Theophrastus (*Plant Research* 7.12.1) says this sort is 'named for its use', but this is a fat lot of help for identifying, or understanding, 'Epimenides' squill'.

54 P.20.97–101, with just one magic dodge attributed to the mythical ('sixth-century BCE') hippie guru (101). All manner of far-out Greek teachings traded under his name.

55 Another jotting from Theophrastus (*Plant Research* 7.13.8).

56 Pliny merges Theophrastus' list with A.N.O.'s – or others' (*Plant Research* 7.13.9).

57 Palestrina near Rome, and the hinterland of Rheims.

58 In 98-9, Pliny sticks *fairly* close to Theophrastus (*Plant Research* 7.2.7).

59 From Theophrastus (*Plant Research* 7.3.1).

60 Though 'shallots' *are* named after Askalon, these aren't shallot bulbs, but some sort of garlic. Theophrastus knows his onions, and will be Pliny's excerpted, garbled, interpolated, mainstay (*Plant Research* 7.4).

61 *Schizo* in Greek means 'divide' (so Theophrastus, *Plant Research* 7.4.7-8).

62 Issus in south-east Anatolia, Sardis in Iran. (Here Pliny translates Theophrastus, *Plant Research* 7.4.9.)

63 Amiternum again – still near Naples.

64 Nero was the all-acting-singing-dancing emperor when Columella finished writing; Pliny took cover (54-68. Cf. Preface, p. 21).

65 Pliny here misreads Greek *prasion* as *prason* (horehound as leek), in translating Theophrastus (*Plant Research* 6.2.5).

66 Mela is unknown; Tiberius again, emperor 14-37. Pliny is buying – and selling – another tall story.

67 We can only say that Pliny lists a Menander in his 'index of books read' for his books 19-21, 23-7. But – is he right?

68 i.e. between (a movable point around) 1-5 January and 17(-23) December. C.11.3.23, above, and Pall. 13.3, our final item, below, both have garlic sowing in December, so this is the right period. Is Pliny looking back from the new year, from latest to earliest optimal dates?

69 This, along with the last point (the age of seed), translates more Theophrastus (*Plant Research* 7.7.6); 117 is after ibid. 7.1.3, and much of 119-23 copies out items from 7.2-3.

70 This is from Theophrastus (ibid. 7.6.3), but Pliny renders *manophullon* as if *monophullon* ('one leaf' for 'lush, bushy leaf').

71 Obviously right. But not true.

72 Only Dr Antonius Musa's prescription stands between Rome's first emperor, on his deathbed at the outset of his reign in the early 20s BCE, and cancellation of the Caesars. Only Pliny's note on doctors' orders stands between Aemilius and oblivion. The world of lettuce!

73 P.20.58.

74 P.20.73, 21.88.

75 On the coast north of the Bay of Naples.

76 The expert on Pliny's and all Roman botany, Jacques André, drily points out that this surprising note is less surprising if we take into account, as Pliny could not, that he has been misidentifying *raphanos* in Theophrastus throughout as '(horse) radish', not 'cabbage' (e.g. in 19.80 ~ *Plant Research* 7.4.4. See *Further Reading: Pliny*).

77 Cato, *Farming* 157.1-2; P.20.78.

78 The early first-century writer on cuisine (lost) M. Gavius Apicius became Rome's proverbial gourmand under the emperors Augustus and Tiberius. Drusus Iulius Caesar (13 BCE-23) died before he could inherit the world empire.

79 Don't try this at home. The 'trefoil' here mistranslates an instruction to wait until the seedling is 'three leaved' before its soda bath, or salt shower (*Geoponica* 12.17.1).

80 See the penultimate note.

81 This is all we know of this story of Civil War Over, from 46-45 BCE (Julius had (counter-)besieged Pompey's – Rome's – troops at Dyrrachium in 49/48 BCE).

82 P.16.173; Cato, *Farming* 161: paraphrased here at 147–9.

83 Yet more from Tiberius, emperor 14–37, and from Germany.

84 Cato, *Farming* 161: his *next to* last thing, in our texts.

85 P.16.173, 19.54.

86 7 March ('Ninth day' back from the Ides of March, May, July, October is the 7th. In other months the 5th).

87 21 April.

88 'Eat cress' in Greek – *not* 'common' in the Greek *we* have. (Not in the Greek proverb collections.)

89 *Gaius* Cornelius Cethegus was consul in 197 BCE and *T.* Quin*c*tius Flamini*n*us was consul in 198 (and busy away liberating Greece through 198–7), their colleagues were two quite other worthies, so Pliny, his unique informant, and his scribes should all rue this aside?

90 *Apium* here is celery, not parsley (cf. Chapter 1, n. 9).

91 The youngest of the four big Greek festivals of games.

92 P.2.108, 18.227.

93 The text is mutilated in our manuscripts.

94 This is from Thebes *in Egypt*. Cummin will next carpet Carpetania in southern *Spain*.

95 This is Theophrastus' fault (*Plant Research* 7.6.3, 9.1.3–4).

96 But he does *not* accept that alexanders grew from myrrh (ibid. 9.1.3–4).

97 11 November.

98 P.13.127.

99 Both areas of south-west Anatolia. The derivation from 'Caria' is bogus.

100 The early first-century Greek court botanist of King Mithridates VI of Pontus (lost).

101 i.e. bread fit for the cereal goddess to eat.

102 From *rheo*, 'flow (i.e. shed petals)'. This makes it the flow-er among flowers!

103 P.20.198.

104 As promised (at P.19.50, above), the last King of Rome shows the son who would never succeed him how to succeed in keeping a throne: strange gardening.

105 'Pederasty' – deeply rooted in all departments of Greek culture (but extant, with *this* referent, only in this Latin text).

106 P.8.99, cf. 20.254.

107 P.13.124.

108 Alabanda and Mylasa were both in Caria, south-west Anatolia; Rosea in upland central Italy.

109 P.13.123.

110 The dog days start on 2 August.

111 The notes to 178 will interrupt paraphrase of Theophrastus in 177 and 179 (*Plant Research* 7.5.4).

112 This late first-century BCE *On Gardening*, from the stable of Augustus' oldest counsellor, also graced by Virgil, Horace, and other great poets, is quite lost, and this is his sole mention.

113 'Forever-living', *semperuiuum* (stonecrop?).

114 Close translation *en bloc* in 181 from Theophrastus, *Plant Research* 7.5.5–6; then, in 181–4, from 7.5.1–3, 7.6.1.

115 A tragic loss, this lost poem must have come up marvellously.

116 Pure Theophrastus – and, after the poetry intrusion, implanted here as such ('are perceived as such . . .': *Plant Research* 7.6.1).

117 Pliny thinks back to his orchard at 15.106. This chapter blends Theophrastus, *Plant Research* 1.12.1–2 with his *Aetiology of Plants* 6.10.1.

118 P.12.127.

CHAPTER 4: A YEAR IN THE GARDEN

1 This over-compresses (garbles) C.11.3.10.

2 This is reported at second-hand from the precepts trading under the seminal philosopher's name, cf. *Geoponica* 5.50.

3 In a lost work of the Platonizing philosopher, novelist, sophist, rhetorician, wizard, and second-century polymath.

4 C.11.3.24.

5 C.11.3.30.

6 The sixth-century encyclopedic Cassiodorus (1.28.6) tells us that this third-century Roman writer 'wrote most beautifully *On Gardens* – the same author whose hard work set out *Feed, Veg., and their Best Points*'. He was an important quarry for Palladius, who quotes him on cucumber (here) and basil (5.3.4, below); we have several scrappy fragments, on peaches, and other orchard fruits (see Maire (2002) in *Further Reading: General*).

7 C.11.3.53.

8 Traditional verbal skirting round menstruation.

9 See 4.9.7–9 above for Gargilius Martialis.

10 At 5.3.1–2, above.

11 At 8.2.1–3, above.

12 This may be a ghost 'radish': is Palladius led by the nose, up Pliny's garden path? (See Chapter 3, n. 47 above.)

13 28 October.

14 At 3.24.9, above.

FURTHER READING

Where next

(1) THE TEXTS

M. Nisard, ed. and French trans., *Les Agronomes Latins* (Paris, 1877)

R. Reitzenstein, ed. *De Scriptorum Rei Rusticae Libris Deperditis* (Berlin, 1884)

A. Richlin, 'Pliny's brassière', in J.P. Hallett and M.B. Skinner, eds *Roman Sexualities* (New Jersey, 1997) 197–220 (esp. 202–4, on women harming plants, in Columella and Pliny)

Virgil, *Georgics*

J.S. Clay, 'The old man in the garden', in T.M. Falkner and J. de Luce, eds *Old Age in Greek and Latin Literature* (New York, 1981) 183–94

C. Day Lewis, trans. (London, 1940)

C.G. Perkell, 'On the Corycian farmer of Virgil's Fourth *Georgic*', *Transactions of the American Philological Association* 111 (1981) 167–77

P. Thibodeau, 'The old man and his garden (*Verg. Georg. 4, 116–48)*', *Materiali e Discussioni* 47 (2001) 175–95

R.F. Thomas, ed. and comm., Vols 1–2 (Cambridge, 1988)

—— 'The old man revisited: memory, reference, and genre in Virgil *Georgics* 4.116–48', in *Reading Virgil and his Texts. Studies in Intertextuality* (Ann Arbor Michigan, 1999) 173–205

Columella, *On Country Life*

H.B. Ash, E.S. Forster, and E.H. Heffner, eds and trans., Vols 1–3 (Loeb Classical Library, Cambridge, Mass., and London, 1955)

F. Boldrer, ed., Italian trans., comm., *L. Iuni Moderati Columellae Rei Rusticae Liber Decimus (Carmen de Cultu Hortorum)* (Pisa, 1996)

E.J. Gowers, 'Vegetable love: Virgil, Columella, and garden poetry', *Ramus* 29 (2000) 127–48

J. Henderson, 'Columella's living hedge: the Roman gardening book', *Journal of Roman Studies* 92 (2002) 110–33

V. Lundström, Å. Josephson, and S. Hedberg, eds *L. Iuni Moderati Columellae Opera Quae Exstant*, 1–8 (Uppsala, 1897–1968)

L.B. Marshall, *L'Horticulture antique et le Poème de Columelle* (Paris, 1918)

R. Martin, 'État présent des études sur Columelle', *Aufstieg und Niedergang der römisches Welt* II.32.3 (1985) 1959–79

E. de Saint-Denis, ed., French trans., and comm., *De l'Agriculture, Livre X* (Collection Budé, Paris, 1969)

—— 'Réhabilitons Columella poète', *Giornale Italiano di Filologia* 31 (1969) 121–36

P. Toohey, 'Gardening with god: Columella', in *Epic Lessons. An Introduction to Ancient Didactic Poetry* (London and New York, 1996) 176–9

Pliny the Elder, *Natural History*

J. André, ed., French trans., and comm., *Histoire Naturelle, Livre XIX* (Collection Budé, Paris, 1964)

M. Beagon, *Roman Nature. The Thought of Pliny the Elder* (Oxford, 1992) esp. 79–91, 'Man and nature in harmony: Pliny on gardens'

J. Henderson, 'Knowing someone through their books: Pliny on Uncle Pliny (*Epistles* 3.5)', *Classical Philology* 97 (2002) 256–84

J. Linderski, '*Imago hortorum*: Pliny the Elder and the gardens of the urban poor', *Classical Philology* 96 (2001) 305–8

T.M. Murphy, *Pliny the Elder's* Natural History: *the Empire in the Encyclopedia* (Cambridge, 2003)

H. Rackham and W.H.S. Jones, eds and trans., Vols 1–10 (Loeb Classical Library, Cambridge, Mass., and London, 1952)

A. Wallace-Hadrill, 'Pliny the Elder and man's unnatural history', *Greece & Rome* 37 (1990) 80–96

Palladius, *Work of Farming*

B. Lodge, trans., *On Husbandrie* (London, 1873)

R. Martin, *Palladius Traité d'Agriculture* Tome Premier (Livres I et II) (Collection Budé, Paris, 1976)

R.H. Rodgers, ed. *Opus Agriculturae* (Bibliotheca Teubneriana, Leipzig, 1975)

(2) GENERAL

J. André, *Lexique des Termes de Botanique en Latin* (Paris, 1956)

M. Beard, 'Imaginary *horti*: or up the garden path', in M. Cima and E. La Rocca, eds *Horti Romani. Atti del Convegno Internazionale. Roma, 4–6 maggio 1995* (Rome, 1998) 21–32

M.T. Boatwright, 'Luxuriant gardens and extravagant women: the *horti* of Rome between Republic and Empire', in M. Cima and E. La Rocca, eds *Horti Romani* (Rome, 1988), 71–82

A. Dalby, *Cato on Farming, De agricultura. A Modern Translation with Commentary* (Totnes, 1998)

L. Farrar, *Ancient Roman Gardens* (Stroud, 1998)

A.S. Gratwick, 'A matter of substance: Cato's preface to the *De agri cultura*', *Mnemosyne* 55 (2002) 41–72

P. Grimal, *Les Jardins Romains* (Paris, 1943; 3rd edn 1984)

W.F. Jashemski, *The Gardens of Pompeii, 1–2* (New Rochelle, 1979, 1993)

J. Lawson, 'The Roman garden', *Greece & Rome* 19 (1950) 97–105

B. Maire, ed. and comm., *Gargilius Martialis. Les remèdes tirés des légumes et des fruits* (Paris, 2002)

S. Pugh, *Garden-Nature-Language* (Manchester, 1988)

N. Purcell, 'Town in country and country in town', in E.B. MacDougall, ed. *Ancient Roman Villa Gardens* (Washington, D.C., 1987) 187–203

—— 'The Roman garden as a domestic building', in I.M. Barton, ed. *Roman Domestic Buildings* (Exeter, 1996) 121–51

W.T. Stearn, *Botanical Latin: History, Grammar, Style, Syntax, Terminology, and Vocabulary* (London, 1966)

H.-D. Stoffler, *Der HORTVLVS des Walahfrid Strabo. Aus dem Kräutergarten des Klosters Reichenau* (Stuttgart, 2001)

W.-D. Storl, *Der Kosmos im Garten. Gartenbau nach biologischen Naturgeheimnissen als Weg zur besseren Ernte* (Aarau, 2001)

F. Waquet, *Latin, Or the Empire of a Sign: from the Sixteenth to the Twentieth Centuries* (London and New York, 2001) esp. 93–5 on botany and Linnaeus

K.D. White, 'Roman agricultural writers', *Aufstieg und Niedergang der römisches Welt* I.4 (1973) 539–97

—— *Country Life in Classical Times* (London, 1977)

—— *Roman Farming* (London, 1970)

DATE CHART

As and when

[BCE]

c. 370–285	Theophrastus, Peripatetic philosopher at Athens: *Research into Plants* 1–9, *Aetiology of Plants*, 1–6, etc. (in Greek)
341–270	Epicurus, Greek philosopher teaching (in garden) at Athens (fragments of hedonist theory survive)
late third-century	Pseudo-Democritus (the early fifth-century philosopher; in Greek), *Georgics*, *On Sympathy and Antipathy*, etc. Ghosted by Bolus of Mendes (a Pythagorean philosopher from Egypt, writing in Greek)
c. third to first century	Aristomachus (of Soloi?; lost Greek writer, *On Apiculture, Wine to Keep*, etc.)
234–149	M. Porcius **Cato**, 'The Censor', *On Agriculture*
?	Menander, *Biochresta* (*Tips for Living*: lost; in Greek)
early first century	Crateuas, Greek botanist at court of Mithridates VI of Pontus (lost)
116–27	M. Terentius **Varro**, *World of the Countryside* 1–3 (37 BCE)

143

70–29	P. Vergilius Maro (**Virgil**), *Georgics* 1–4 (29 BCE)
late first century	Sabinus Tiro, *On Gardening* (lost)
late first century	C. Iulius Hyginus, *World of the Countryside* (lost)

[CE]

early first century	M. Gavius Apicius, writer on cuisine (lost)
mid first century	Moschion, lost Greek medical writer, wrote *On the Radish*, on cabbage, cosmetics
fl. c. 60	L. Iunius Moderatus **Columella**, *World of the Countryside* 1–12
23/24–79	C. Plinius Secundus (**Pliny the Elder**), *Natural History* 1–37 (*c.* 77)
c. 120–80	Apuleius, *World of the Countryside* (lost)
early third century	Q. Gargilius Martialis, *On Gardens* (few fragments survive, on fruit)
c. 361	Vindanius Anatolius of Beirut, *Sunagoge Georgikon Epitedeumaton* 1–12 (*Excerpts on Farming Practice*: lost; in Greek)
late fourth century	**Palladius**, *The Work of Agriculture* 1–15
c. sixthtenth centuries	*Geoponica, or Cassianus Bassus the scholar's* Excerpts on *The World of the Countryside*, 1–20, revised for Emperor Constantine VII Porphyrogenitus of Byzantium (in Greek)
c. 830	Walahfrid Strabo, *On Horticulture* (poem in 444 hexameters on a herb garden in a German Benedictine monastery)

144

INDEXES

NAMES AND VARIETIES

(1) THE PLANTS:

ENGLISH NAMES

(Latin where identification is in doubt)

acanthus (bearsfoot) 29
black alexanders – olusatrum 7, 8, 10, 38, 42, 56, 95, 100
all-heal – panaces 6, 37, 40, 55, 100; panax 95
alum, see [wild] garlic
amaranth – amaranthus 57, 129
anise – anesum 96, 100, 113, 117
armoracia, see [wild] radish 76, 122
artichoke – carduus, cinara 6, 37, 43, 59, 63, 69, 92, 110, 113, 119, 122–3
arum (dragon-root) 59, 79, 130
Askalon, see shallot
asparagus – asparagus 25, 37, 43, 59, 63, 69, 91–2, 112, 115–6
[wild] asparagus, see corruda
balsam – (opo)balsamum 61, 114
[pearl] barley – tisana 99
basil – ocimum 6, 40–1, 61, 80, 84–6, 93–4, 98–9, 109, 118–9, 123
[Egyptian] bean – colocasium 113–4, 119
eye bean – phaselus 63
bearsfoot – acanthus 59
beet – beta (nigra) 7, 38, 43, 60, 62, 77, 80, 83–5, 88–9, 99, 112, 114, 119, 121–2
[pale] beet – b. alba 62
blackthorn – spinus 30
blite spinach – blitus 80, 84–6, 117
bramble – rubus, uepris 29, 32, 46, 53, 59, 73
briar, see bramble

[dogs] briar, dog-rose? – sentis canis, kunosbatos 32
broccoli, see cabbage
[butchers] broom – ruscus 9, 63
[black] bryony – bryonias, t(h)amnus 59
[white] bryony – psilothrum, uitis alba 9, 105, 107, 131
bulb – bulbus 79–80, 85
bunias (French turnip) – 64, 131
cabbage – brassica, caulis, olus 6, 9, 27, 37, 39, 43, 62, 69–70, 75, 88–91, 96, 98, 106, 110, 112, 114, 117–21, 129, 133, 135
[wild] cabbage – olus siluestre 91
caper – capparis 7, 9, 38, 46–7, 56, 95, 114, 118, 121–2
caraway – careum 95
cardoon thistle – carduus 69, 92–3, 113
carrot – pastinaca 7, 129
[wild] carrot – 9
cassia – cas(s)ia 61
celandine – glaucium 55
celery 7, 9, 29, 94, 124; see parsley
centaury – centaureum 100
chervil – chaerophyllum 7, 37, 43, 56, 97, 117, 121
chick-pea – cicer 98, 100, 105
chicory – cichoreum, intibum 56, 87
chives – porrum sectile 6, 10, 40–1, 43, 63, 82, 112–13
[sweet] cicely – myrrhis 57, 129
colocynth – 107
coramble – 57, 129

145

LATIN NAMES

Keyed to the entries in the Index of English Names.
L. = Linnaeus classification

(2) GENERAL TOPICS: